Introduction to Easy, Quick Family Meals

Easy One-Dish Meals is all about helping everyone who cooks do it in less time and really enjoy the results.

The importance of family meals is well known. Family meals do much to keep families together, to enrich lives and to instill healthy values and habits.

Easy One-Dish Meals makes it easy to plan, to cook and to serve families and friends. All the ingredients are readily available in your own pantry, refrigerator or the familiar shelves in your regular grocery store. Meals are easy when you start with easy recipes and an easy plan.

Most recipes do not need anything to go with them. Others are even better with a "bag salad" and bread from your own refrigerator or the grocery store.

Do your part to enrich the lives of people around you. Serve a homecooked meal today!

Table of Contents

Easy Beautiful Brunches

Breakfast Frittata

2 medium zucchini, diced, dried
1 cup finely diced fresh mushrooms   240 ml
2 ripe avocados, peeled, cubed
5 eggs
1½ cups shredded Swiss cheese   360 ml

- Cook zucchini and mushrooms in large skillet with a little oil over medium heat for 4 to 5 minutes or just until tender. Remove from heat and sprinkle with a little salt and pepper.

- Place cubed avocado over top of vegetable mixture. Beat eggs and about 1 cup (240 ml) water or milk until frothy and pour over ingredients in skillet.

- Return skillet to medium heat, cover and cook 5 minutes or until eggs set. Top with cheese, cover and cook 1 minute more or just until cheese melts. Cut in wedges to serve.

Corned Beef Hash-n-Eggs

1 (15 ounce) can corned beef hash   425 g
1 (11 ounce) can Mexicorn, drained   312 g
4 eggs
¾ cup chili sauce   180 ml

- Preheat oven to 375° (190° C). Spread corned beef hash in greased 9-inch (23 cm) pie pan and spoon corn over hash.

- With large spoon, make 4 depressions in corn and break 1 egg in each depression. Spoon chili sauce over top of eggs. Bake for 20 minutes or until eggs set.

Bacon & Eggs Anyone?

This brunch casserole is also great for a late night supper. You really don't need anything else with it except biscuits or toast.

2 potatoes, peeled, cubed	
¼ cup (½ stick) plus 3 tablespoons butter, melted	60 ml; 45 ml
¼ cup flour	60 ml
1 pint half-and-half cream	.5 kg
1 (16 ounce) package shredded cheddar cheese	.5 kg
1 teaspoon dried Italian seasoning	5 ml
12 hard-boiled eggs, sliced	
1 pound bacon, cooked, slightly crumbled	.5 kg
1½ cups breadcrumbs	360 ml

- Cook potatoes in salted water just until tender, but do not overcook. Drain well.

- In large saucepan melt ¼ cup (60 ml) butter and stir in flour. Cook, stirring constantly, 1 minute or until smooth.

- Gradually add cream and cook over medium heat, stirring constantly, until sauce thickens. Add cheddar cheese, Italian seasoning, salt and white pepper to taste, stirring constantly, until cheese melts. Remove from heat.

- In buttered 9 x 13-inch (23 x 33 cm) baking dish, layer half egg slices, half bacon and half cheese sauce. Spoon potatoes over cheese sauce and top with remaining egg slices, bacon and cheese sauce.

- Combine breadcrumbs and 3 tablespoons (45 ml) melted butter. Sprinkle over top of casserole. Cover and refrigerate overnight.

- Before baking remove casserole from refrigerator and let stand for about 20 minutes. Uncover and bake at 350° (176° C) for 30 minutes.

Fiesta Eggs

1 pound sausage	.5 kg
½ green bell pepper, chopped	
½ red bell pepper, chopped	
3 green onions, chopped	
1 (10 ounce) can tomatoes and green chilies	280 g
½ cup hot, chunky salsa	120 ml
4 ounces cubed processed cheese	114 g
10 eggs, slightly beaten	
½ cup sour cream	120 ml
⅔ cup milk	160 ml

- Slowly brown sausage, bell peppers and onions in skillet. Spoon sausage-onion mixture onto paper towels, drain and set aside.

- Dry skillet with more paper towels, pour tomatoes, green chilies, salsa and processed cheese in skillet and cook, stirring constantly, only until cheese melts. Remove from heat.

- In bowl beat eggs, 1½ teaspoons (7 ml) salt, sour cream and milk and fold in sausage mixture and tomato-cheese mixture. Transfer to greased 7 x 11-inch (18 x 30 cm) baking dish.

- Bake uncovered at 325° (162° C) for about 25 minutes or until center is set.

Breakfast Tortillas

¾ cup chopped onion	180 ml
¼ cup (½ stick) butter	60 ml
¼ cup flour	60 ml
¾ cup milk	180 ml
1 pint half-and-half cream	480 ml
1 (7 ounce) can chopped green chilies	198 g
10 eggs	
3 avocados	
8 (8-inch) flour tortillas	8 (20 cm)
1 (8 ounce) package shredded Monterey Jack cheese	227 g

- Preheat oven to 350° (176° C). Saute onion in butter in large skillet. Stir in flour, cook on low 1 minute and stir constantly. Add milk and cream, cook on medium heat and stir constantly until mixture thickens.

- Add green chilies, garlic powder and ½-1 teaspoon (2-5 ml) each of salt and pepper. Remove sauce from heat and set aside.

- In another skillet, scramble eggs lightly and remove from heat. In small bowl, mash avocados and sprinkle with a little salt.

- Spread tortillas on counter and dip 2 tablespoons (30 ml) of sauce, one-eighth of eggs and one-eighth of avocados on each tortilla. Roll and place seam-side down on greased 9 x 13-inch (23 x 33 cm) baking dish. Spoon remaining sauce over tortillas.

- Bake covered for about 25 minutes or just until tortillas are hot and bubbly. Remove from oven, sprinkle cheese over top and return to oven for about 10 minutes. When serving, top each tortilla with a dab of salsa if desired.

Quick Breakfast Sandwiches

Wouldn't the kids love to say they had sandwiches for breakfast!
What a cool Mom!

8 slices white bread*	
Butter, softened	
2 cups cooked, finely chopped ham	480 ml
1 cup shredded Swiss cheese	240 ml
3 eggs, beaten	
1⅔ cups milk	400 ml
1 tablespoon dried, minced onion flakes	15 ml
1 teaspoon prepared mustard	5 ml

- Trim crusts off bread slices. Spread butter on 1 side of each slice of bread. Place 4 slices in buttered 8-inch (20 cm) square baking pan.

- Top bread slices with chopped ham and remaining bread slices, buttered side up. Sprinkle with shredded Swiss cheese.

- In bowl combine eggs, milk, onion flakes, prepared mustard and about ½ teaspoon (2 ml) salt and mix well. Slowly pour over bread slices. Cover and refrigerate overnight or at least 8 hours.

- Remove baking pan from refrigerator about 10 minutes before cooking. Bake uncovered at 325° (162° C) for 30 minutes or until center sets. To serve, cut into 4 sandwiches.

TIP: Use regular bread slices, not thin sandwich slices.

English Muffin
Breakfast Sandwich

4-6 eggs
1 (12 ounce) package English muffins, halved,   340 g
    toasted
1 (16 ounce) package pre-cooked bacon slices,   .5 kg
    halved
1 (16 ounce) package cheese slices   .5 kg

- Prepare eggs in skillet over medium heat and stir often. Season according to taste.

- Heat bacon in microwave according to package directions. Spoon egg mixture onto bottom of muffin, add cheese slice, bacon and muffin top.

Breakfast-Cinnamon Cake

⅔ cup packed brown sugar   160 ml
1 tablespoon grated orange peel   15 ml
2 (12 ounce) refrigerated cinnamon rolls   2 (340 g)

- Preheat oven to 375° (190° C). Coat 1 (10-inch/25 cm) bundt pan with cooking spray.

- In small bowl, combine brown sugar and orange peel. Open cans of rolls (save icing), cut each in quarters and coat each with cooking spray.

- Dip in sugar-orange mixture and arrange evenly in bundt pan. Gently press down on each. Bake 35 minutes until light brown and about double in size.

- Cool slightly in pan. Invert serving plate on top of pan, hold plate and pan together with oven mitts and invert. Remove pan. Spread icing unevenly over top of cake and serve warm.

Overnight Breakfast

*This is "French toast" the easy way and it's not just
for company! The kids will love it too.*

7 cups small cubed French bread, bottom crust removed	1.6 ml
¾ cup chopped pecans	180 ml
1 (3 ounce) package cream cheese, softened	84 g
4 tablespoons sugar	60 ml
1 (8 ounce) carton whipping cream	227 g
½ cup real maple syrup	120 ml
6 eggs, slightly beaten	
1 teaspoon vanilla	5 ml
½ teaspoon ground cinnamon	2 ml

- Place cubed bread in greased 9 x 13-inch (23 x 33 cm) baking dish and press down gently. Sprinkle with pecans.

- In mixing bowl, beat cream cheese and sugar until fluffy and gradually mix in whipping cream and syrup.

- In separate bowl whisk eggs, vanilla, cinnamon and about ½ teaspoon (2 ml) salt and fold into cream cheese-whipping cream mixture.

- Slowly pour this mixture evenly over bread. Cover and refrigerate overnight.

- Remove from refrigerator 20 minutes before baking. Bake covered at 350° (176° C) for 30 minutes or until center sets and top is golden brown. To serve, cut into squares and serve with maple syrup.

Croissant French Toast with Strawberry Syrup

4 large day-old croissants
¾ cup half-and-half cream — 180 ml
2 large eggs
1 teaspoon vanilla — 5 ml
¼ cup (½ stick) butter — 60 ml

- Slice croissants in half lengthwise. In shallow bowl, whisk cream, eggs and vanilla. Heat 1 tablespoon (15 ml) butter at a time in large skillet.

- Dip croissant halves into egg mixture and coat well. Cook about 2 minutes, 4 croissant halves at a time, turn and cook on both sides until light brown.

- Repeat procedure with remaining butter and croissant halves.

Strawberry Syrup:
1 quart fresh strawberries, sliced — 1 L
¾ cup sugar — 180 ml
¼ cup orange juice — 60 ml

- Combine all ingredients for syrup in saucepan and let stand 30 minutes.

- Cook over low to medium heat, stirring occasionally, for 5 to 8 minutes. Serve warm over Croissant Toast.

Orange-French Toast

1 egg, beaten	
½ cup orange juice	120 ml
5 slices raisin bread	
1 cup crushed graham crackers	240 ml
2 tablespoons butter	30 ml

- Combine egg and orange juice.

- Dip each slice of bread in egg mixture and then in graham cracker crumbs.

- Fry in butter until brown.

Cherry-Pecan Oatmeal

2 cups of your favorite oatmeal, cooked	480 ml
½ cup dried cherries, chopped	120 ml
½ cup packed brown sugar	120 ml
¼ cup (½ stick) butter, softened	60 ml
½ teaspoon ground cinnamon	2 ml
½ cup chopped pecans, toasted	120 ml

- Cook your favorite oatmeal. Combine cherries, brown sugar, butter and cinnamon. Stir into cooked oatmeal.

- Spoon into individual serving bowls and sprinkle toasted pecans over top of each serving.

Eggs in A Basket

2 (15 ounce) cans corned beef hash	2 (425 g)
6 eggs	
¼ cup seasoned breadcrumbs	60 ml
Butter	

- Preheat oven to 325° (162° C). Grease 7 x 11-inch (18 x 28 cm) baking dish and spread hash evenly in dish. Press bottom of ½-cup (120 ml) measuring cup into hash to make 6 impressions.

- Break 1 egg into each impression. Sprinkle spoonful of breadcrumbs over each egg and top with dot of butter. Bake 20 to 25 minutes or until eggs are as firm as desired.

Heavenly Eggs for The Saints

Bread and butter
Eggs
Mozzarella cheese slices
Precooked bacon slices, heated

- Preheat oven to 350° (176° C). Butter slice of bread for each person and place buttered side down in baking dish. Place cheese slice over bread.

- Separate 1 egg for each slice of bread. Add pinch of salt to egg whites and beat until stiff.

- Pile egg whites on cheese and make nest in top. Slip 1 egg yolk into each nest and bake 20 minutes. Serve immediately.

- Cut cooked bacon in half and lay pieces over eggs like a cross. Serve immediately.

Breakfast Shake

1 banana, cut into 1-inch slices
1 mango, peeled, cubed
1½ cups pineapple juice or orange juice, chilled   360 ml
1 (8 ounce) container vanilla yogurt   227 g

- Process banana slices, mango, juice and yogurt in blender until smooth. Scrape sides of blender and mix. Serve immediately.

No-Mess Oven Pancakes

⅔ cup flour   160 ml
⅔ cup milk   160 ml
¼ cup sugar   60 ml
5 large eggs, beaten

- Preheat oven to 425° (220° C). Combine flour, milk, sugar and beaten eggs in mixing bowl. Place a little oil on large baking sheet and rub oil to cover whole surface of pan. Place in oven for 5 minutes to heat.

- Pour pancake mixture onto pan to make several pancakes. Bake about 18 minutes or until puffy and golden.

- Serve with maple syrup and fresh berries.

Easy
Super
Salads

Zesty Bean Salad

1 (15 ounce) can kidney beans	425 g
1 (15 ounce) can pinto beans	425 g
1 (16 ounce) package frozen whole kernel corn, thawed, drained	.5 kg
1 red onion and 1 bell pepper, seeded, chopped	
1 (7 ounce) can chopped green chilies	198 g
2 cups cubed deli ham	480 ml

- Rinse and drain kidney beans and pinto beans and place in salad bowl. Add corn, onion, bell pepper, green chilies, cubed ham and mix well.

Dressing:

1 (8 ounce) bottle cheddar-parmesan ranch dressing	227 g
2 tablespoons lemon juice	30 ml

- Pour ranch dressing into small bowl and stir in lemon juice. Pour over salad and toss. Refrigerate several hours before serving for flavors to blend.

Easy Vegetable Salad

1 head cauliflower
1 head broccoli
1 (10 ounce) package frozen green peas, thawed   280 g
2 ribs celery, diagonally sliced
1 bunch fresh green onion, sliced
2 cups cubed deli ham   480 ml

- Wash and drain cauliflower and broccoli and break into florets. Place in large mixing bowl. Add peas, celery, green onions, cubed ham and toss.

Dressing:

2 cups mayonnaise   480 ml
¼ cup sugar   60 ml
1 tablespoon white vinegar   15 ml
1 cup shredded mozzarella cheese   240 ml

- Combine all dressing ingredients and pour over vegetables and toss. Chill several hours before serving.

Green-Rice Salad

1 (10 ounce) package mixed baby salad greens	280 g
2 cups cooked rice, chilled	480 ml
2 (11 ounce) cans mandarin oranges,	
well drained, chilled	2 (312 g)
½ cup thinly sliced scallions, chilled	120 ml

- Combine salad greens, rice, oranges and scallions in salad bowl.

Dressing for Green-Rice Salad:

1 (8 ounce) bottle Italian salad dressing	227 g
1 teaspoon ground cumin	5 ml
1 avocado, peeled, well mashed	

- In jar with lid, combine salad dressing, cumin, avocado, ½ teaspoon (2 ml) each of salt and pepper. Pour about half the dressing over salad and toss. Add more as needed.

Harmony Salad

2 heads red leaf lettuce, torn	
2 (11 ounce) cans mandarin oranges, drained	2 (312 g)
2 avocados, peeled, cubed	
1 red onion, sliced	
¼ cup sunflower kernels	60 ml
Red wine vinaigrette dressing	

- In salad bowl, place lettuce, oranges, avocados and onion slices and refrigerate.

- Use a pint jar with lid to combine all dressing ingredients and shake well to mix. When ready to serve, shake dressing again, drizzle over salad and toss. Sprinkle sunflower kernels over top of salad.

Fruit and Greens Delight

2 (10 ounce) bags radicchio salad mix	2 (280 g)
2 golden delicious apples, cored, cut in wedges	
1¼ cups crumbled blue cheese	300 ml
⅔ cup chopped walnuts	160 ml

• Combine all salad ingredients in salad bowl.

Apple Vinaigrette Dressing:

⅔ cup applesauce	160 ml
⅓ cup olive oil	80 ml
⅓ cup cider vinegar	80 ml
1 tablespoon dijon-style mustard	15 ml

• Combine vinaigrette dressing ingredients in small bowl and mix well. Toss with salad.

*TIP: If you slice the apples several minutes before serving, sprinkle
1 tablespoon or so (15 ml) lemon juice over them and
toss so they will not turn dark.*

Pasta Toss

1 (8 ounce) package bow-tie pasta	227 g
2 cups diagonally sliced carrots	480 ml
2 cups broccoli florets	480 ml
1 red and 1 yellow bell pepper	
2 cups cubed ham	480 ml

- Cook pasta according to package directions. Drain pasta and add 1 tablespoon (15 ml) olive oil and cool.

- Add carrots, broccoli, bell peppers and cubed ham.

Dressing:

¾ cup creamy Italian salad dressing	180 ml
2 tablespoons balsamic vinegar	30 ml
1 tablespoon sugar	15 ml

- Combine dressing ingredients plus ½ teaspoon (2 ml) each of salt and pepper. Pour over vegetables and toss. Chill several hours before serving.

Super Summer Salad Supreme

⅓ pound cooked deli roast beef	168 g
1 (15 ounce) can 3-bean salad, chilled, drained	425 g
1 (8 ounce) block mozzarella cheese, cubed	227 g
1 (10 ounce) bag mixed salad greens with Italian dressing	280 g

- In large salad bowl, lightly toss beef, 3-bean salad and cheese. Pour in just enough salad dressing to moisten greens.

*TIP: Substitute turkey or ham for beef and
Swiss cheese for mozzarella.*

Pasta and Lemon Pea Salad

1 pound bow-tie pasta	.5 kg
1 (10 ounce) package frozen baby green peas, thawed	280 g
½ cup mayonnaise	120 ml
2 tablespoons lemon juice	30 ml
½ cup whipping cream	120 ml
2 cups cubed ham	480 ml

- Cook pasta as according to package directions. Add peas in last 2 minutes of cooking time. Drain pasta and peas, rinse in cold water and drain again.

- Transfer to large salad bowl. Combine mayonnaise with lemon juice, 1 teaspoon (5 ml) salt, a little pepper and stir in cream and cubed ham.

- Fold mayonnaise mixture into pasta and peas and toss to coat well. Refrigerate several hours before serving.

Gourmet Couscous Salad

1 (10 ounce) box chicken-flavored couscous	280 g
2 tomatoes, coarsely chopped	
2 zucchini, coarsely chopped	
4 fresh green onions, sliced	
1 cup crumbled feta cheese	240 ml
1 cup cubed deli turkey	240 ml

- Cook couscous according to package directions, but do not use butter.

- In salad bowl combine tomatoes, zucchini, green onions, cubed turkey and couscous.

Dressing:

1 tablespoon lemon juice	15 ml
¼ cup olive oil	60 ml
½ teaspoon dried basil	2 ml

- Combine dressing ingredients plus ½ teaspoon (2 ml) pepper in pint jar with lid and shake until they blend well.

- When ready to serve, add feta cheese, pour dressing over salad and toss. Refrigerate.

Italian Salad

1 (10 ounce) package mixed salad greens	280 g
1 cup shredded mozzarella cheese	240 ml
1 (2 ounce) can sliced ripe black olives	57 g
1 (15 ounce) can cannelloni beans, rinsed and drained	425 g

- In salad bowl, combine greens, cheese, olives and well drained cannelloni beans. Toss with Zesty Italian salad dressing.

- Serve with Italian bread and cheeses if you like.

Rainbow Pasta Salad

1 (16 ounce) package tri-color spiral pasta	.5 kg
1 red and yellow bell pepper, thinly sliced	
4 small zucchini with peel, sliced	
3 ribs celery, sliced diagonally	

- Cook pasta according to package direction, rinse in cold water and drain well. In large bowl, combine pasta, bell peppers, zucchini and celery.

Dressing:

1 (14 ounce) can sweetened condensed milk	396 g
1 cup white vinegar	240 ml
1¼ cups mayonnaise	300 ml

- Combine condensed milk, vinegar, mayonnaise and 2 teaspoons (10 ml) pepper in small bowl. Pour dressing over salad. Toss well, cover and refrigerate overnight.

- Serve over bed of lettuce with breadsticks.

Chunky Egg Salad

12 hard-cooked eggs, quartered
⅓ cup sun-dried tomato gourmayo   80 ml
2 ribs celery, sliced
½ cup sliced, stuffed green olives   120 ml

- Place all ingredients in salad bowl and add salt and pepper to taste.

- Gently toss and serve over bed of lettuce leaves with crackers.

TIP: *This is also great stuffed in hollowed-out tomato, bell pepper or melon. And if you are really in a hurry, just put it between 2 slices of dark bread.*

Spinach Salad

1 (10 ounce) bag baby spinach   280 g
1 cup fresh sliced strawberries   240 ml
1 (3 ounce) package silvered almonds, toasted   85 g
½ cup crumbled feta cheese   120 ml

- Combine all ingredients in salad bowl and toss with Poppy Seed Vinaigrette.

Poppy Seed Vinaigrette Dressing:
½ cup sugar   120 ml
¼ cup white wine vinegar   60 ml
⅓ cup olive oil   80 ml
2 teaspoons poppy seeds   10 ml

- Combine all ingredients and toss with spinach mixture.

Toss the Greens

1 (10 ounce) package mixed salad greens	280 g
1½ cups halved cherry tomatoes	360 ml
1 cucumber, sliced	
1 red onion, sliced in rings	
1 pound seasoned, cooked chicken breasts, cut into strips	.5 kg

Dressing:

Prepared Italian salad dressing	
Lots of seasoned black pepper	
¼ teaspoon cayenne pepper	1 ml

- Combine greens, tomatoes, cucumber and onion rings in large salad bowl and toss. When ready to serve, toss with salad dressing.

- Arrange salad on individual salad plates, top with strips of chicken and sprinkle with lots of pepper and cayenne pepper.

TIP: Keep your salads crisper longer by chilling the salad plates or serving bowls.

Super Summer Salad

1 (10 ounce) box uncooked orzo pasta	280 g
1 (10 ounce) package frozen broccoli florets	280 g
1 (10 ounce) package frozen green beans	280 g
1 (12 ounce) jar baby corn nuggets, drained	340 g
2 cups cooked, cubed ham	480 ml

Dressing:

1 (8 ounce) jar sweet-and-sour sauce	227 g
2 tablespoons olive oil	30 ml

- Cook orzo in large saucepan according to package directions. Stir in broccoli and green beans 5 minutes before orzo is done.

- Boil and cook additional 5 minutes. Drain well. Transfer pasta and vegetables to salad bowl and add corn and ham. Sprinkle with 1 teaspoon (5 ml) salt, pour on sweet-and-sour sauce and olive oil and toss.

Chicken-Caesar Salad

4 boneless, skinless chicken breast halves, grilled	
1 (10 ounce) package romaine salad greens	280 g
½ cup shredded parmesan cheese	120 ml
1 cup seasoned croutons	240 ml

- Cut chicken breasts into strips. Combine chicken, salad greens, cheese and croutons in large bowl.

- When ready to serve, toss with ¾ cup (180 ml) Caesar or Italian salad dressing.

Friday-After-Thanksgiving Salad

2 (10 ounce) packages prepared romaine lettuce	2 (280 g)
2½-3 cups cooked, sliced turkey	600-710 ml
1 (8 ounce) jar baby corn, quartered	227 g
2 tomatoes, chopped	
1 (8 ounce) package shredded colby cheese	227 g

- In large salad bowl, combine romaine lettuce, turkey, baby corn, tomatoes and cheese.

Dressing:

⅔ cup mayonnaise	160 ml
⅔ cup prepared salsa	160 ml
¼ cup cider vinegar	60 ml
2 tablespoons sugar	30 ml

- Combine all dressing ingredients in bowl and mix well.

- When ready to serve, sprinkle on a little salt and pepper, pour dressing over salad and toss to coat well.

*TIP: If you want to make this leftover dish an even
"bigger and better" salad, just add some ripe olives,
red onion, black beans or the pre-cooked bacon.*

Fiesta Holiday Salad
This is great for that leftover holiday turkey!

1 (10 ounce) package torn romaine lettuce	280 g
3 cups diced smoked turkey	710 ml
1 (15 ounce) can black beans, rinsed, drained	425 g
2 tomatoes, quartered, drained	

- Combine lettuce, turkey, beans and tomatoes in large salad. Combine mayonnaise and salsa.

Dressing:

⅔ cup mayonnaise	160 ml
¾ cup prepared salsa	180 ml

- When ready to serve, spoon dressing over salad and toss. If you like, a sliced red onion can be added to salad.

TIP: For a little extra touch, you might sprinkle crumbed bacon over top of salad. You can buy the real, cooked, crumbled bacon in the grocery store if you don't have time to fry some.

One of the good things about salads is that you can use ingredients you have on hand. If you start with 1-2 bags of greens, you can add any of the following items you may have in the pantry. The list of ingredients is much longer than this list, so be creative: Green beans, pinto beans, red kidney beans, black beans, green olives, ripe olives, corn, many canned vegetables, crackers, nuts, seeds, pasta, rice. Check the refrigerator for perishables and add them to your salad as well.

Supper-Ready Beef and Bean Salad

¾ pound deli roast beef, cut in strips	340 g
2 (15 ounce) can kidney beans, rinsed, drained	2 (425 g)
1 cup chopped onion	240 ml
1 cup chopped celery	240 ml
3 hard-boiled eggs, chopped	

- Combine beef strips, beans, onion, celery and chopped eggs in salad bowl.

Dressing:

⅓ cup mayonnaise	80 ml
⅓ cup chipotle-chili gourmayo	80 ml
¼ cup ketchup	60 ml
¼ cup sweet pickle relish	60 ml
2 tablespoons olive oil	30 ml

- In small bowl, combine mayonnaise, chipotle-chili gourmayo, ketchup, pickle relish and oil and mix well.

- Spoon over beef-bean mixture and toss. Refrigerate several hours before serving.

- Rather than serving in salad bowl, shred lettuce on serving plate and serve beef-bean salad over lettuce.

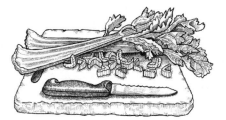

Colorful Salad Toss

2 (8 ounce) packages baby spinach,
   stems removed   2 (227 g)
1 small head cauliflower, cut into small florets
1 sweet red bell pepper, cut in strips
¾ cup whole walnuts   180 ml
½ cup roasted sunflower seeds   120 ml
2 cups chopped ham   480 ml
Berry vinaigrette salad dressing

- In large salad bowl, combine spinach, cauliflower, bell pepper strips, walnuts, chopped ham, sunflower seeds and a generous amount of salt.

- Toss with strawberry or raspberry vinaigrette salad dressing.

Beefy Green Salad

⅓ pound cooked deli roast beef   168 g
1 (15 ounce) can 3-bean salad, chilled, drained   425 g
½ pound mozzarella cheese, cubed   227 g
1 (8 ounce) bag mixed salad greens
   with Italian dressing   227 g

- Cut beef in thin strips. In large salad bowl, lightly toss beef, 3-bean salad and cheese. Pour in just enough salad dressing to moisten greens.

TIP: Substitute turkey or ham for beef and
Swiss cheese for mozzarella.

Fruited Pork Salad Lunch

Salad:

1 (10 ounce) package fresh green salad mix	280 g
2 cups halved, seedless green grapes	480 ml
1 cup fresh strawberries	240 ml
1 cup refrigerated red grapefruit sections	
with juice	240 ml

Pork:

½-¾ pound cooked pork tenderloin,	
thinly sliced, chilled	227-340 g

Dressing:

¼ cup juice from grapefruit sections	60 ml
2 tablespoons red wine vinegar	30 ml
2 tablespoons oil	30 ml
1 teaspoon poppy seeds	5 ml
2 teaspoons honey	10 ml

- Toss salad mix, green grapes, strawberries and grapefruit sections in salad bowl.

- Arrange salad on individual plates and place tenderloin slices over top.

- Mix all dressing ingredients well and pour dressing over top of salads.

Grilled Chicken with Broccoli Slaw

Chicken:

1 (3½ pound) chicken, quartered	1.5 kg
3 tablespoons olive oil	45 ml
⅔ cup bottled barbecue sauce	160 ml

- Brush chicken quarters with oil and sprinkle with a little salt and pepper.

- Grill 30 to 35 minutes and turn once or twice until juices run clear when thigh part is pierced and meat thermometer registers 170° (76° C) when inserted into chicken.

- Brush with barbecue sauce and grill just until sauce browns, but do not char.

Slaw:

¼ cup mayonnaise	60 ml
3 tablespoons cider vinegar	45 ml
2 tablespoons sugar	30 ml
1 (12 ounce) package broccoli slaw	340 g

- Combine mayonnaise, vinegar and sugar and mix well. Spoon over broccoli slaw and toss. Refrigerate until ready to serve.

Strawberry-Chicken Salad

1 pound boneless, skinless chicken breast halves	.5 kg
1 (10 ounce) package spring greens mix	280 g
1 pint fresh strawberries, sliced	.5 kg
½ cup chopped walnuts	120 ml

Dressing:

¾ cup honey	180 ml
⅔ cup red wine vinegar	160 ml
1 tablespoon soy sauce	15 ml
½ teaspoon ground ginger	2 ml

- Cut chicken into strips and place in large skillet with a little oil. Cook on medium to high heat for about 10 minutes and stir occasionally.

- While chicken cooks, combine all dressing ingredients and mix well. After chicken strips cook for 10 minutes, pour ½ cup (120 ml) dressing into skillet with chicken and cook 2 minutes longer or until liquid evaporates.

- In salad bowl, combine spring greens mix, strawberries and walnuts, pour on remaining dressing and toss. Top with chicken strips.

Hawaiian-Chicken Salad

3 cups cooked, diced chicken breasts	710 ml
1 (20 ounce) can pineapple tidbits, well drained	567 g
1 cup halved red grapes	240 ml
1 cup chopped celery	240 ml
1 large banana	

- Combine diced chicken, pineapple, grapes and celery and toss. Cover and refrigerate.

Dressing:

¾ cup mayonnaise	180 ml
½ cup poppyseed dressing	120 ml
½ cup salted peanuts	120 ml

- Combine mayonnaise, poppyseed dressing and a sprinkle of salt for dressing.

- When ready to serve, slice bananas and add to salad.

- Top with mayonnaise-poppyseed dressing and toss. Just before serving, sprinkle peanuts over top of salad.

Barbecue-Chicken Salad

Here's a quickie with that "it-takes-a-long-time" flavor.

Dressing:

¾ cup ranch dressing	180 ml
3 tablespoons prepared barbecue sauce	45 ml
2 tablespoons salsa	30 ml

- Combine all dressing ingredients, chill and set aside.

Salad:

3 grilled boneless, skinless chicken breast halves	
1 (9 ounce) package romaine lettuce	255 g
1 (15 ounce) can seasoned black beans, rinsed, drained	425 g
12-15 cherry tomatoes	

- Cut chicken breasts in strips and in oven just enough to warm thoroughly.

- Place chicken strips, cut-up romaine, black beans and cherry tomatoes. Toss with enough dressing to lightly coat.

TIP: The next time you grill, just grill some extra chicken breasts and freeze them to use for this dish. Or, if you don't have time to grill chicken, just use deli smoked turkey.

Black Bean Chicken Salad

3 to 4 boneless, skinless chicken breast halves,
  cooked, cubed
1 (15 ounce) can black beans, drained   425 g
1 bunch green onions, chopped
1 cup chopped celery   240 g

Cumin-Vinaigrette Dressing:
¾ cup virgin olive oil   180 ml
¼ cup lemon juice   60 ml
2 teaspoons dijon-style mustard   10 ml
2 teaspoons ground cumin   10 ml

- Combine chicken, black beans, onions and celery.

- Combine all dressing ingredients and mix well.

- Pour dressing over black bean-chicken salad, toss and
  chill.

*Olive oil is the Mediterranean's "liquid gold" and is used quite freely
for all Italian cooking. The two most common varieties of olive are
extra-virgin or "light" and olive oil or "dark." Extra-virgin olive oil
is better suited for salads and marinades rather than cooking.*

Apple-Walnut Chicken Salad

3 to 4 boneless, skinless chicken breast halves,
   cooked, cubed
2 tart green apples, peeled, chopped
½ cup chopped pitted dates   120 ml
1 cup finely chopped celery   240 ml

Dressing:
½ cup chopped, toasted walnuts   120 ml
⅓ cup sour cream   80 ml
⅓ cup mayonnaise   80 ml
1 tablespoon lemon juice   15 ml

- Combine chicken, apples, dates and celery.

- Toast walnuts at 300° (148° C) for 10 minutes.

- Combine sour cream, mayonnaise and lemon juice and
  mix well. Add in walnuts.

- Pour dressing over chicken salad and toss. Chill.

Tarragon-Chicken Salad

1 cup chopped pecans	240 ml
3 - 4 boneless, skinless chicken breast halves, cooked, cubed	
1 cup chopped celery	240 ml
¾ cup peeled, chopped cucumbers	180 ml

- Place pecans in shallow pan and toast at 300° (148° C) for 10 minutes.

- Combine chicken, celery and cucumbers.

Dressing:

⅔ cup mayonnaise	160 ml
1 tablespoon lemon juice	15 ml
2 tablespoons tarragon vinegar	30 ml
1¼ teaspoons crumbled, dried tarragon	6 ml

- Combine all dressing ingredients and mix well.

- When ready to serve, toss with chicken mixture and add pecans.

Southwestern Chicken Salad

4 cups cubed, cooked chicken breasts	1 kg
1 (16 ounce) can black beans, drained	.5 kg
¾ red onion, chopped	
½ red bell pepper and ½ yellow bell pepper, chopped	
¼ cup chopped fresh cilantro	60 ml
½ cup sour cream	120 ml
¼ cup mayonnaise	60 ml
½ teaspoon garlic powder	2 ml
1 jalapeno pepper, seeded, finely chopped	
1 teaspoon lime juice	5 ml
½ cup pine nuts, toasted	120 ml

- Combine chicken, beans, onion, bell peppers and cilantro in large bowl.

- Whisk sour cream and mayonnaise in small bowl.

- Stir in garlic powder, jalapeno pepper and lime juice and add to chicken. Add a little salt and pepper to taste and toss.

- Chill at least 1 hour. Just before serving, toss in pine nuts. Serve on bed of lettuce. Serves 8.

Mexican Chicken Salad

3-4 boneless, skinless chicken breast halves, cooked, cubed	
1 (15 ounce) can chick-peas, drained	425 g
1 red and 1 green bell pepper, seeded, diced	
1 cup chopped celery	240 ml

- Combine all ingredients and serve with dressing below.

Dressing for Mexican Chicken Salad:

1½ cups sour cream	360 ml
2 tablespoons chili sauce	30 ml
2 teaspoons ground cumin	10 ml
1 small bunch cilantro, minced	

- Combine all ingredients for dressing and add a little salt and pepper.

- Pour over chicken salad and toss. Chill before serving.

Spinach-Turkey Salad Supper

2 (8 ounce) packages baby spinach	2 (227 g)
⅓ cup whole walnuts	80 ml
⅓ cup craisins	80 ml
2 red delicious apples with peel, sliced	
¾ pound deli smoked turkey	340 g
Honey-mustard salad dressing	

- In large salad bowl, combine spinach, walnuts, craisins, apples and turkey.

- Toss with ½ cup (120 ml) prepared honey-mustard salad dressing.

Noodle-Turkey Salad

1 (3 ounce) package oriental-flavor ramen noodle soup mix	84 g
1 (16 ounce) package finely shredded coleslaw mix	.5 kg
¾ pound deli smoked turkey, cut into strips	340 g
½ cup prepared vinaigrette salad dressing	120 ml

- Coarsely crush noodles and place in bowl with lid. Add coleslaw mix and turkey strips.

- Combine vinaigrette salad dressing and seasoning packet from noodle mix in small bowl.

- Pour over noodle-turkey mixture and toss to coat mixture well. Refrigerate.

Chicken-Grapefruit Salad Supper

1 (10 ounce) package romaine salad mix	280 g
1 (24 ounce) jar grapefruit sections, well drained	680 g
1 rotisserie chicken, boned, cubed	
½ red onion, sliced	

Dressing:

2 tablespoons orange juice	30 ml
2 tablespoons white wine vinegar	30 ml
2 tablespoons extra-virgin olive oil	30 ml

- Combine salad mix, well drained grapefruit sections, chicken and onion in salad bowl.

- In small bowl, combine all dressing ingredients plus 1 teaspoon (5 ml) each of salt and pepper, pour over salad and toss.

Bridge Club Luncheon Favorite

1 rotisserie-cooked chicken	
1 cup red grapes, halved	240 ml
1 cup green grapes, halved	240 ml
2 cups chopped celery	480 ml
⅔ cup whole walnuts	160 ml
⅔ cup sliced fresh onion	160 ml

- Skin chicken and cut chicken breast in thin strips. (Save dark meat for another meal or use frozen, grilled chicken breasts.) Place in bowl with lid.

- Add red and green grapes, celery, walnuts and sliced onions.

Dressing:

½ cup mayonnaise	120 ml
1 tablespoon orange juice	15 ml
2 tablespoons red wine vinegar	30 ml
1 teaspoon chili powder	5 ml

- Combine all dressing ingredients, add a little salt and pepper to taste and mix well.

- Spoon over salad mixture and toss. Refrigerate.

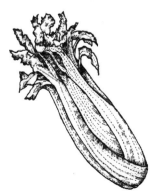

Herbed-Chicken Salad

1 rotisserie-cooked chicken	
¼ cup chopped fresh chives	60 ml
2 tablespoons capers	30 ml
1 cup chopped celery	240 ml
1 cup chopped sweet pickles	240 ml

- Skin chicken and cut meat from bones. Slice chicken in thin strips and place in bowl.

- Add fresh chives, capers, celery and sweet pickles and mix well.

Dressing:

¼ cup extra-virgin olive oil	60 ml
3 tablespoons white wine vinegar	45 ml
1 teaspoon chopped fresh thyme	5 ml
1 teaspoon oregano	5 ml
1 tablespoon honey	15 ml

- Whisk olive oil, vinegar, thyme, oregano, honey and a little salt and pepper to taste in bowl. Spoon over chicken salad and toss. Refrigerate.

Old-Fashioned
Chicken or Turkey Salad

3 cups cooked, cubed chicken or turkey	710 ml
⅔ cup chopped celery	160 ml
¾ cup sweet pickle relish	180 ml
1 bunch fresh green onions with tops, chopped	
3 hard-boiled eggs, chopped	
¾ cup mayonnaise	180 ml

- Combine chicken, celery, relish, onions and eggs.

- Toss with mayonnaise and chill. Serve on lettuce leaf.

Fancy Chicken or Turkey Salad

3 cups cooked, cubed chicken or turkey	710 ml
1 cup chopped celery	240 ml
1½ cups halved green grapes	360 ml
¾ cup cashew nuts	180 ml
¾ cup mayonnaise	180 ml
1 cup chow mein noodles	240 ml

- Combine chicken, celery, grapes and cashew nuts and toss with mayonnaise.

- Just before serving, mix in noodles and serve on cabbage left.

Chicken and Rice Salad

3 cups cooked, cubed chicken or turkey	710 ml
1 (6 ounce) box long-grain, wild rice, cooked, drained	168 g
1 bunch fresh green onions with tops, chopped	
1 cup chopped walnuts	240 ml
1 (8 ounce) can sliced water chestnuts	227 g
1 cup mayonnaise	240 ml
¾ teaspoon curry powder	4 ml

- Combine chicken, rice, onions, walnuts and water chestnuts. Toss with mayonnaise and curry powder and chill. Serve on bed of lettuce.

Wacky Tuna Salad

1 (7 ounce) package cooked, light tuna in water	198 g
1 red apple with peel, cored, chopped	
1 (10 ounce) package frozen green peas, thawed, drained	280 g
1 sweet red bell pepper, chopped	

Dressing:

½ (8 ounce) bottle sweet honey Catalina salad dressing	½ (227 g)
½ cup mayonnaise	120 ml

- Place tuna in bowl, add chopped apple, green peas and bell pepper and mix well.

- Combine dressing and mayonnaise, pour over tuna salad and stir to blend well.

- Refrigerate at least 2 hours and serve over bed of shredded lettuce.

Tuna-Tortellini Salad

1 (7 ounce) package cut spaghetti	198 g
¼ cup (½ stick) butter	60 ml
1 (12 ounce) can tuna, drained	340 g
1 (4 ounce) can sliced ripe olives	114 g

Dressing:

¾ cup whipping cream	180 ml
1 teaspoon dried basil leaves	5 ml
2 tablespoons parmesan cheese	30 ml
1 teaspoon seasoned salt	5 ml

- Cook spaghetti according to package directions and drain. Add butter and stir until butter melts. Add tuna and olives.

- Combine whipping cream, basil, cheese and seasoned salt for dressing. Pour over spaghetti-tuna mixture and toss.

Supper-Ready Shrimp Salad

1 (14 ounce) package frozen, cooked tortellini, thawed	396 g
1 pound cooked, peeled, veined shrimp	.5 kg
½ cup sliced ripe olives	120 ml
½ cup chopped celery	120 ml
½ cup zesty Italian salad dressing	120 ml

- Combine tortellini, shrimp, olives and celery in salad bowl.

- Pour salad dressing over salad and toss. Serve immediately or refrigerate until ready to serve.

Easy
Sassy
Sandwiches

Hot Roast Beef Sandwich

1 (12 ounce) loaf French bread	340 g
¼ cup creamy dijon-style mustard	60 ml
¾ pound sliced deli roast beef	340 g
8 slices American cheese	

- Preheat oven to 325° (162° C).

- Split French bread and spread mustard on bottom slice.

- Line slices of beef over mustard and cheese slices over beef with cheese on top.

- Cut loaf in quarters and place on baking sheet.

- Heat for about 5 minutes or until cheese just partially melts.

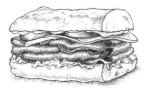

Reuben Sandwiches

12 slices dark rye bread	
6 slices Swiss cheese	
12 thin deli slices corned beef	
4 cups deli coleslaw, drained	1 L

- On 6 slices of rye bread, layer cheese, 2 slices corned beef and lots of the coleslaw.

- Top with remaining bread slices.

A Different Sandwich

Dressing:
½ cup mayonnaise	120 ml
⅓ cup dijon-style mustard	80 ml
¼ cup prepared horseradish	60 ml

Bread:
6 (7 inch) Italian focaccia flatbreads	6 (18 cm)

• Combine dressing ingredients in small bowl. Use serrated knife to slice bread shells in half horizontally.

Ingredients:
1 pound deli-shaved roast beef	.5 kg
1 (12 ounce) jar roasted red bell peppers, cut in strips	340 g
6 slices mozzarella cheese	
Baby romaine lettuce	

• Spread generous amount dressing on one side of bread.

• Top with several slices roast beef, roasted peppers, cheese, romaine and remaining bread half.

• To serve, cut sandwiches in half.

TIP: You know, this recipe is not exact science. If you don't have horseradish, mayonnaise will be fine. Sharing the meal with the family and friends is the most important thing.

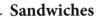

Tasty Sub Sandwich

4 (6-inch) sub rolls   4 (15 cm)

Filling:
1 onion, halved, thinly sliced
2 tablespoons butter   30 ml
2 tablespoons beef granules   30 ml
8 sliced deli roast beef
4 slices provolone cheese

- Slice rolls in half lengthwise, place on baking sheet and broil until golden brown. Preheat oven to 350° (176° C).

- Cook onion with a little oil in skillet on low to medium heat for 6 minutes. Set aside.

- Heat butter, ½ cup (120 ml) water and beef granules in saucepan. Use tongs to dip beef slices into hot liquid.

- Place beef slices and cheese slices on bottom of 4 rolls. Divide cooked onion over cheese and place top rolls over onions.

- Place filled sub rolls on baking sheet and heat for 5 minutes or just until cheese melts.

Southwest Burgers

You will need a package of 8 kaiser buns for these Southwest burgers.

2 pounds lean ground beef	1 kg
1 packet taco seasoning mix	
1 cup salsa, divided	240 ml
8 slices hot pepper jack cheese	

- Combine beef, taco seasoning and ¼ cup (60 ml) salsa in large mixing bowl. Shape mixture into 8 patties.

- If you are grilling, cook patties about 12 minutes or until they cook thoroughly and turn once.

- To broil in oven, place patties on broiler pan 4 to 5 inches from heat and broil until they cook thoroughly. Turn once during cooking.

- When patties are almost done, place buns cut side down on grill and heat 1 or 2 minutes.

- Place 8 patties on bottom half of buns, top with cheese and cook an additional 1 minute or until cheese melts.

- Top with heaping tablespoon salsa and top half of bun.

It's A Tortilla Wrap

2 large (9 inch) garden spinach tortillas   23 cm
Mayonnaise

- Heat broiler, place tortillas on baking sheet and broil briefly on each side.

- Remove from oven and spread thin layer of mayonnaise over 1 side of tortillas.

Filling:
1 cup shredded cheddar cheese   240 ml
1 (9 ounce) package spring salad mix   255 g
1 cup diced tomatoes   240 ml
4 finely chopped green onions
6 slices thin deli turkey or ham

- Spread cheese over tortillas and return to oven just until cheese melts.

- Combine salad mix, tomatoes and green onions and sprinkle on tortillas. Place 3 slices of turkey or ham on tortillas. Roll up or fold over to wrap them up.

Open-Face Apple-Ham Sandwiches

*You will need some kaiser rolls or whatever you have
in the pantry for these sandwiches.*

Mayonnaise and mustard
8 thin slices deli, boiled ham
1 red delicious apple with peel, finely chopped
16 slices American cheese

- Spread a little mayonnaise and mustard on top and
  bottom of 4 kaiser rolls and place on baking sheet.

- Top each with 1 slice cheese, 1 slice ham and about
  2 tablespoons (10 ml) chopped apple. Top with
  remaining slices of cheese.

- Broil 4 to 5 inches from heat just until top slice of cheese
  melts. Serve immediately.

Wrap It Up Now!

4 burrito-size flour tortillas
¼ cup sweet-honey Catalina dressing   60 ml
4 slices deli ham
4 slices Swiss cheese
1½ cups deli coleslaw   360 ml

- Spread tortillas with dressing and add 1 slice ham and
  1 slice cheese on each tortilla. Spoon one-fourth of
  coleslaw on top.

- Roll up and wrap each in wax paper. Place in
  microwave and heat just until cheese melts. Cut wraps
  in half to serve.

A Special Grilled Cheese Sandwich

Make as many of these sandwiches as you need. Just multiply the ingredients below by the number you need.

1 loaf 7-grain bread
Butter, softened

Filling for 1 sandwich:

2 tablespoons gourmayo with chipotle	30 ml
2 slices sharp cheddar cheese	
2 tablespoons real crumbled bacon	30 ml
¼ whole avocado, thinly sliced	

- For each sandwich, spread softened butter on 2 thick slices of 7-grain bread. Place 1 slice, butter side down, in heavy skillet.

- Spread with 1 tablespoon (15 ml) gourmayo and 1 slice cheese.

- Sprinkle with 2 tablespoons (30 ml) crumbled bacon and avocado slices. Top with second slice of cheese and remaining slice of bread spread with 1 tablespoon (15 ml) gourmayo.

- Heat skillet on medium to high and cook about 2 minutes or until light brown and cheese melts.

- Turn sandwich over and cook another 2 minutes or until cheese melts completely.

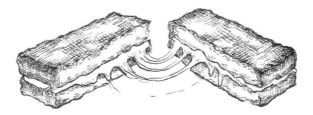

A Family Sandwich

1 (8 ounce) loaf French bread	227 g
1 (11) ounce) bottle creamy dijon-gourmayo	312 g
6 ounces sliced Swiss cheese	168 g
6 ounces sliced deli-sliced ham	168 g
8 sandwich-sliced dill pickles	

- Preheat oven to 350° (176° C). Cut bread in half horizontally and spread dijon-gourmayo over cut sides of bread.

- Arrange half of cheese and half of ham on bottom slice and top with pickle slices. Spread remaining cheese and ham on top of pickles.

- Cover with top of bread, press down on sandwich and cut into quarters. Place on cookie sheet and bake 5 minutes. Serve hot.

Sunday Night Chicken Sandwiches

1 (10 ounce) package frozen breaded chicken breast patties	280 g
½ (12 ounce) carton guacamole dip	½ (340 g)
⅓ cup thick, chunky salsa	80 ml
½ (9 ounce) package shredded lettuce	½ (255 g)
4 whole wheat hamburger buns, split	

- In skillet with a very little oil, cook breaded chicken breast patties according to package directions.

- Spread thin layer of guacamole dip on bottom of each bun, top each with chicken patty and spread salsa on top of patty. Place 3 to 4 tablespoons (45-60 ml) shredded lettuce over salsa. Spread another thin layer of guacamole on top bun and place over each filled bottom bun.

Italian-Sausage Sandwiches

1 pound sweet Italian sausage	.5 kg
1 red bell pepper, chopped	
1 onion, chopped	
1⅔ cups Italian-style spaghetti sauce	400 ml

- Remove casing from sausage and cook sausage, bell pepper and onion in skillet over medium heat or until sausage browns.

- Stir in spaghetti sauce and heat until boiling. Simmer for 5 minutes and stir constantly. Pour mixture over split hoagie rolls.

Confetti Sandwiches

1 tablespoon lemon juice	15 ml
1 (8 ounce) package cream cheese, softened	227 g
½ cup grated carrots	120 ml
¼ cup each grated cucumber, purple onion	
and bell pepper	60 ml

- Combine lemon juice with cream cheese and add enough mayonnaise to make cheese into spreading consistency.

- Fold in grated vegetables, spread on bread for sandwiches and chill.

"Honey Do"
Open-Face Sandwich

4 kaiser rolls, split
⅓ cup prepared honey-mustard dressing   80 ml
8 thin slices deli honey ham
8 slices Swiss cheese

- Preheat oven to 400° (204° C).

- Spread honey-mustard on each split roll. Top each with ham and cheese slices.

- Place on baking sheet and bake 4 to 5 minutes or until cheese melts.

Meatball Heros

Any bread like club rolls, hot dog buns or French rolls will work.

1 (16 ounce) container marinara sauce   .5 kg
1 (16 ounce) package frozen bell peppers,
   thawed   .5 kg
½ onion, minced
1 (12 ounce) package cooked Italian meatballs 340 g

- Combine marinara sauce, bell peppers and onion and cook in large saucepan on medium heat for 5 minutes.

- Add meatballs, cover and gently boil for about 5 minutes or until meatballs are hot.

- Spoon into split club rolls and serve hot.

Wrap-That-Turkey Burger

1 pound ground turkey	.5 kg
⅓ cup shredded 4-cheese blend	80 ml
¼ cup finely grated, drained onion	60 ml
1 teaspoon Creole spicy seasoning	5 ml

Wrap:

4 fajita-size flour tortillas, warmed	
⅔ cup prepared guacamole	160 ml
2 cups shredded lettuce	480 ml

- Combine ground turkey, shredded cheese, grated onion and spicy seasoning in bowl.

- Shape into 4 patties (make patties a little longer than round) and refrigerate about 30 minutes before cooking.

- Grill patties about 5 inches from heat for about 8 minutes or until thermometer reads 165° (75° C).

- Place tortillas on flat surface and arrange one-fourth lettuce on each tortilla.

- Place 1 patty on each tortilla and spread with guacamole. Fold tortilla in half to cover filling.

TIP: If you don't want to buy spicy seasoning, use 1 teaspoon (5 ml) seasoned salt and ¼ teaspoon (1 ml) cayenne pepper.

Chicken Sandwich Olé

1 (10 ounce) package frozen breaded
   chicken breast patties   280 g
½ cup prepared black bean dip   120 ml
⅓ cup thick and chunky hot salsa   80 ml
Lettuce, shredded
Tomatoes, chopped

- Preheat oven to 325° (162° C).

- Heat chicken breast patties in oven according to package directions. Place 4 split hoagie buns in oven the last 3 minutes of cooking time.

- Spread bottom half of each hoagie liberally with bean dip and salsa. Top each with chicken patty, shredded lettuce and chopped tomatoes.

- Place top bun over lettuce and tomatoes. Serve immediately.

Fruited Chicken Salad

1 (10 ounce) package spring salad mix   280 g
1 (6 ounce) package frozen, ready-to-serve
   chicken strips, thawed   168 g
½ cup fresh strawberries and raspberries 120 ml
½ fresh peach, sliced

Dressing:
1 (8 ounce) bottle raspberry salad dressing   227 g

- In salad bowl, combine salad mix, chicken strips, berries and peach. Toss with just enough salad dressing to coat salad. Put on 7-grain bread or serve on a bed of lettuce with bread, crackers or breadsticks.

Walnut-Cream Sandwiches

2 (8 ounce) packages cream cheese, softened	2 (227 g)
½ cup mayonnaise	120 ml
1 teaspoon dijon-style mustard	5 ml
6 slices bacon, cooked, crumbled	
¾ cup finely chopped walnuts	180 ml

- In mixing bowl, beat cream cheese, mayonnaise and mustard until creamy.

- Fold in bacon and chopped walnuts and mix well.

- Spread on pumpernickel or rye bread and slice in thirds.

Crab-Avocado Burgers

4 hamburger buns	
4 prepared frozen crab cakes	
1 ripe avocado	
¼ cup mayonnaise	60 ml
1 tablespoon lemon juice	15 ml
1 (4 ounce) can green chilies, drained	114 g

- Microwave crab cakes according to package directions.

- Mash avocado, mayonnaise, lemon juice and ½ teaspoon (2 ml) salt together with fork. Stir in green chilies.

- Place crab cakes on buns and spread with avocado-mayonnaise mixture. Serve as is or top with lettuce and sliced tomatoes.

B L T Tortilla Wraps

Flour tortillas	Cooked bacon
Mayonnaise	Lettuce, shredded
Sliced turkey	Tomatoes, chopped

- Spread each tortilla with mayonnaise with 2 slices turkey, 2 slices bacon and shredded lettuce and tomatoes.

- Fold edges over to enclose filling. Serve immediately or wrap in wax paper and refrigerate.

Seafood Tortilla Wraps

2 large (9 inch) garden spinach tortillas   23 cm
Mayonnaise

- Heat broiler, place tortillas on baking sheet and broil very briefly on each side.

- Remove from oven and spread mayonnaise on 1 side of tortilla.

Filling:
1 cup shredded American cheese   240 ml
1 (9 ounce) spring salad mix   255 g
1 cup diced tomatoes, drained   240 ml
4 finely chopped green onions
1 (4 ounce) package albacore steak with lemon and
  cracked pepper, crumbled   114 g

- Spread cheese over tortillas and return to oven just until cheese melts.

- Combine salad mix, tomatoes and green onions and sprinkle on tortillas.

- Place as much of the crumbled albacore on tortilla as needed. Roll up or fold over to eat.

Salmon Burgers

Salmon Patties:

1 (15 ounce) can salmon with liquid	425 g
1 egg, slightly beaten	
½ cup lemon juice	120 ml
⅔ cup seasoned breadcrumbs	160 ml

Burgers:

Hamburger buns
Mayonnaise
Lettuce
Sliced tomatoes

- Combine salmon with 2 tablespoons (30 ml) liquid from salmon can, egg, lemon juice, breadcrumbs and a little salt and pepper.

- Form into patties and with a little oil, fry on both sides until golden. Serve hot on buns with mayonnaise, lettuce and sliced tomatoes.

Fish and Chips Sandwiches

1 (12 ounce) box frozen breaded fish fillets, thawed	340 g
1 (8 ounce) loaf Italian bread	227 g
1 cup prepared deli coleslaw	240 ml
4 ounces potato chips	114 g

- Heat fish fillets according to package directions. Remove from oven and preheat broiler.

- Slice bread in half lengthwise and broil, cut side up.

- Layer coleslaw, fish fillets and potato chips and cover with bread tops. To serve, cut into quarters and serve immediately.

Easy
Savory Soups
and Stews

The Ultimate
Cheddar Cheese Soup

You won't believe how good this soup is!

1 cup finely chopped onion	240 ml
1 red bell pepper, diced	
2 tablespoons butter	30 ml
1 pound extra sharp cheddar cheese, grated	.5 kg
2 tablespoons cornstarch	30 ml
1 (14 ounce) can chicken broth	396 g
1½ cups cooked, diced ham	360 ml
1½ cups broccoli florets, cooked	360 ml
¾ cup cooked, diced carrots	180 ml
1 teaspoon Worcestershire sauce	5 ml
½ teaspoon garlic powder	2 ml
2 cups half-and-half cream	480 ml

- Saute onion and bell pepper in butter in large saucepan. Mix cheese and cornstarch.

- Pour broth into saucepan and add cheese-cornstarch mixture a little at a time.

- Cook soup over medium heat until cheese melts. Stir until smooth and creamy.

- Add ham, broccoli, carrots, Worcestershire, garlic powder and a little salt and white pepper to taste and stir well.

- Heat over low heat, pour in cream and stir well. Serves 6 to 8.

Easy Spinach Soup

2 (10 ounce) packages frozen chopped spinach,
   cooked   2 (280 g)
2 (10 ounce) cans cream of mushroom soup   2 (280 g)
1 cup half-and-half cream   240 ml
1 (15 ounce) can chicken broth   425 g

- Place spinach, mushroom soup and half-and-half in blender and puree until smooth.

- Place spinach mixture and chicken broth in saucepan and heat on medium heat until hot.

- Reduce heat to low and simmer for 20 minutes. Serve hot or cold.

Speedy Creamy
Broccoli-Rice Soup

1 (6 ounce) package chicken and wild rice mix   168 g
1 (10 ounce) package chopped broccoli   280 g
2 (10 ounce) cans cream of chicken soup   2 (280 g)
1 (12 ounce) can chicken breast chunks   340 g

- Combine rice mix, seasoning packet and 5 cups (1.3 L) water in soup pot or kettle. Bring to boil, reduce heat and simmer 15 minutes.

- Stir in broccoli, chicken soup and chicken. Cover and simmer for another 5 minutes.

Mexican-Style Minestrone Soup

1 (16 ounce) package frozen garlic-seasoned pasta and vegetables	.5 kg
1 (16 ounce) jar thick and chunky salsa	.5 kg
1 (15 ounce) can pinto beans with liquid	425 g
1 teaspoon chili powder	5 ml
1 teaspoon cumin	5 ml
1 (8 ounce) package shredded Mexican 4-cheese blend	227 g

- Combine pasta and vegetables, salsa, pinto beans, chili powder, cumin and 1 cup (240 ml) water in large saucepan.

- Heat to boiling, reduce heat and simmer for about 8 minutes, stirring occasionally or until vegetables are tender.

- When ready to serve, top each serving with Mexican cheese.

Fiesta Soup

1 (15 ounce) can Mexican-style stewed tomatoes	425 g
1 (15 ounce) can whole kernel corn	425g
1 (15 ounce) pinto beans	425 g
1 (14 ounce) can chicken broth	396 g
1 (10 ounce) can fiesta nacho soup	280 g

- In soup pot or kettle, on high heat, combine tomatoes, corn, pinto beans, chicken broth and a little salt and mix well.

- Stir in nacho soup and heat just until hot. (If you feel that soup needs a touch of meat, just add 1 (12 ounce/340 g) can white chicken chunks.)

*Navy Bean Soup

8 slices thick-cut bacon, divided	
1 carrot	
3 (15 ounce) cans navy beans with liquid	3 (425 g)
3 ribs celery, chopped	
1 onion, chopped	
2 (15 ounce) cans chicken broth	2 (425 g)
1 teaspoon Italian herb seasoning	5 ml
1 (10 ounce) can cream of chicken soup	1 (280 g)

- Cook bacon in skillet, drain and crumble. Reserve 2 crumbled slices for garnish. Cut carrot in half lengthwise and slice.

- Combine most of crumbled bacon, carrot, beans, celery, onion, broth, seasoning, 1 cup (240 ml) water in 5 to 6-quart (5 to 6 L) slow cooker and stir to mix.

- Cover and cook on LOW for 5 to 6 hours. Ladle 2 cups (480 ml) soup mixture into food processor or blender and process until smooth.

- Return to cooker, add cream of chicken soup and stir to mix. Turn heat to HIGH and cook another 10 to 15 minutes.

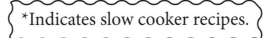

*Indicates slow cooker recipes.

*Black Bean Soup

2 (14 ounce) cans chicken broth	2 (396 g)
3 (15 ounce) cans black beans, rinsed, drained	3 (425 g)
2 (10 ounce) cans tomatoes and green chilies	2 (280 g)
1 onion	
1 teaspoon ground cumin	5 ml
½ teaspoon dried thyme	2 ml
½ teaspoon dried oregano	2 ml
2 to 3 cups finely diced, cooked ham	480 - 710 ml

- In slow cooker, combine chicken broth and black beans and turn cooker to HIGH. Cook just long enough for ingredients to get hot.

- With potato masher, mash about half of beans in slow cooker. Reduce heat to LOW and add tomatoes, green chilies, onion, spices, diced ham and ¾ cup (180 ml) water.

- Cover and cook for 5 to 6 hours.

Easy Meaty Minestrone

2 (10 ounce) cans minestrone soup	2 (280 g)
1 (15 ounce) can pinto beans with liquid	425 g
1 (18 ounce) package frozen Italian meatballs, thawed	510 g
1 (5 ounce) package grated parmesan cheese	143 g

- In large saucepan, combine soups, beans, meatballs and ½ cup (120 ml) water. Bring to boil, reduce heat to low and simmer about 15 minutes. To serve, sprinkle each serving with parmesan cheese.

*Indicates slow cooker recipes.

Mexican Black Bean Soup

2 onions, finely chopped	
3 teaspoons minced garlic	15 ml
3 teaspoons chili powder	15 ml
3 (15 ounce) cans black beans	3 (425 g)
1 teaspoon cumin	5 ml
1 (10 ounce) can beef broth	280 g

- Saute onions in kettle with little oil and cook on medium heat for 5 minutes. Stir in garlic and chili powder.

- Puree 1 can beans and add to onion mixture. Add remaining beans, cumin and beef broth.

- Bring heat to boil, reduce heat and simmer for 10 minutes. When serving, garnish with shredded cheese or salsa.

Southern Turnip Greens Stew

2 (16 ounce) packages frozen chopped turnip greens	2 (.5 kg)
1 (10 ounce) package frozen diced onion and bell peppers	280 g
2 cups chopped, cooked ham	480 ml
1 teaspoon sugar	5 ml
2 (15 ounce) cans chicken broth	2 (425 g)

- Combine turnip greens, onions, bell peppers, ham, sugar, chicken broth and 1 teaspoon (5 ml) black pepper in soup kettle.

- Boil mixture, reduce heat, cover and simmer for 30 minutes.

*Southern Soup

1½ cups dry black-eyed peas	360 ml
2 to 3 cups finely diced, cooked ham	480 - 710 ml
1 (15 ounce) can whole kernel corn	425 g
1 (10 ounce) package frozen cut okra, thawed	280 g
1 onion, chopped	
2 teaspoons Cajun seasoning	10 ml
1 large potato, chopped	
1 (14 ounce) can chicken broth	396 ml
2 (15 ounce) cans Mexican stewed tomatoes	2 (425 g)

- Rinse peas and drain. Combine peas and 5 cups (1.3 L) water in large saucepan.

- Bring to boil, reduce heat, simmer about 10 minutes and drain.

- Combine peas, ham, corn, okra, onion, potato, seasoning, broth in 5 to 6-quart (5 to 6 L) slow cooker.

- Add 2 cups (480 ml) water and mix

- Cover and cook on LOW for 5 to 6 hours. Add stewed tomatoes and continue cooking for 1 more hour.

*Indicates slow cooker recipes.

*Tater Talk Soup

5 medium potatoes, peeled, cubed	
2 cups cooked, cubed ham	480 ml
1 cup fresh broccoli florets, cut very, very fine	240 ml
1 (10 ounce) can cheddar cheese soup	280 g
1 (10 ounce) can fiesta nacho cheese soup	280 g
1 (14 ounce) can chicken broth	396 g
2½ soup cans milk	

- Place potatoes, ham and broccoli in slow cooker sprayed with vegetable cooking spray. In saucepan, combine soups and milk.

- Heat just enough to mix until smooth. Stir into ingredients already in slow cooker. Cover and cook on LOW for 7 to 9 hours. When serving, sprinkle a little paprika over each serving if desired.

*Corn-Ham Chowder

1 (14 ounce) can chicken broth	396 g
1 cup whole milk	240 ml
1 (10 ounce) can cream of celery soup	280 g
1 (15 ounce) can cream-style corn	425 g
1 (15 ounce) can whole kernel corn	425 g
½ cup dry potato flakes	120 ml
1 onion, chopped	
2-3 cups chopped, leftover cooked ham	480 - 710 ml

- In 6-quart (6 L) slow cooker, combine broth, milk, soup, cream-style corn, whole kernel corn, potato flakes, onion and ham.

- Cover and cook on LOW for 4 to 5 hours. When ready to serve, season with salt and pepper.

*Ham-Vegetable Chowder

This is a great recipe for leftover ham.

1 medium potato	
2 (10 ounce) cans cream of celery soup	2 (280 g)
1 (14 ounce) can chicken broth	396 g
2 cups finely diced ham	480 ml
1 (15 ounce) can whole kernel corn	425 g
2 carrots, sliced	
1 onion, coarsely chopped	
1 teaspoon dried basil	5 ml
1 (10 ounce) package frozen broccoli florets	280 g

- Cut potato into 1-inch (2.5 cm) pieces. Combine all ingredients except broccoli florets in large slow cooker.

- Cover and cook on LOW for 5 to 6 hours. Add broccoli, about 1 teaspoon (5 ml) each of salt and pepper to cooker and cook for 1 more hour.

Easy Pork Tenderloin Stew

This is a great recipe for leftover pork or beef.

2-3 cups cubed, cooked pork	710 ml
1 (12 ounce) jar pork gravy	340 g
¼ cup chili sauce	60 ml
1 (16 ounce) package frozen stew vegetables	.5 kg

- In soup pot, combine cubed pork, gravy, chili sauce, stew vegetables and ½ cup (120 ml) water.

- Bring to boiling and boil 2 minutes; reduce heat and simmer for 10 minutes. Serve with cornbread or hot biscuits.

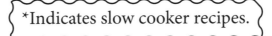
*Indicates slow cooker recipes.

Black Bean Stew Supper

1 (16 ounce) pork and beef sausage ring, thinly sliced	.5 kg
2 onions and 3 ribs celery, chopped	
3 (15 ounce) cans black beans, rinsed, drained	3 (425 g)
2 (10 ounce) cans tomatoes and green chilies	2 (280 g)
2 (14 ounce) cans chicken broth	2 (396 g)

- Place sausage slices, onion and celery in soup kettle with a little oil and cook until sausage is slightly brown and onion is soft. Drain fat.

- Add beans, tomatoes, green chilies and broth. Bring mixture to boiling, reduce heat and simmer for 30 minutes.

- Take out about 2-3 cups (710 ml) soup mixture, place in blender and pulse until almost smooth.

- Return mixture to kettle and stir to thicken stew. Return heat to high until stew is thoroughly hot.

Easy Potato Soup

1 (16 ounce) package frozen hash brown	.5 kg
1 cup chopped onion	240 ml
1 (14 ounce) can chicken broth	396 g
1 (10 ounce) can cream of celery	280 g
1 (10 ounce) can cream of chicken soup	280 g
2 cups milk	480 ml

- Combine potatoes, onion and 2 cups (480 ml) water in large saucepan and bring to boil. Cover, reduce heat and simmer 30 minutes.

- Stir in broth, soups and milk and heat thoroughly. (If you like, garnish with shredded cheddar cheese or diced, cooked ham.)

Polish-Vegetable Stew

1 onion, sliced	
1 carrot, sliced	
2 (15 ounce) cans stewed tomatoes	2 (425 g)
2 (15 ounce) cans new potatoes, quartered	2 (425 g)
1 pound Polish sausage	.5 kg
1 (9 ounce) package coleslaw mix	255 g

- Place a little oil in large soup pot. Cook onion and carrot slices for 3 minutes or until tender-crisp and add tomatoes.

- Cut sausage in 1-inch (1.2 cm) pieces. Add potatoes and sausage to soup mixture.

- Bring to boil, reduce heat and simmer 10 minutes.

- Stir in coleslaw mix, cook another 8 minutes and stir occasionally.

Potato-Sausage Soup

1 pound pork sausage link	.5 kg
1 cup chopped celery	240 ml
1 cup chopped onions	240 ml
2 (10 ounce) cans potato soup	2 (280 g)
1 (14 ounce) can chicken broth	396 g

- Cut sausage in 1-inch (2.5 cm) slices.

- Brown sausage slices in large heavy skillet, drain and remove sausage to separate bowl.

- Leave about 2 tablespoons (30 ml) sausage drippings in skillet and saute celery and onion.

- Add potato soup, ¾ cup (180 ml) water, chicken broth and cooked sausage slices. Bring to boil, reduce heat and simmer for 20 minutes.

Italian Garbanzo Soup

1 (16 ounce) package frozen diced onions and bell peppers	.5 kg
1 pound Italian sausages, sliced	.5 kg
1 (14 ounce) can beef broth	396 g
1 (15 ounce) can Italian stewed tomatoes	425 g
2 (15 ounce) cans garbanzo beans, rinsed, drained	2 (425 g)

- In soup pot with a little oil, sauté onion and bell peppers. Add Italian sausage and cook until brown. Stir in beef broth, stewed tomatoes and garbanzo beans.

- Bring mixture to boil, reduce heat and simmer about 30 minutes.

Quick Spicy Tomato Soup

2 (10 ounce) cans tomato soup	2 (280 g)
1 (16 ounce) can Mexican stewed tomatoes	.5 kg
Sour cream	
½ pound bacon, fried, drained, crumbled	227 g

- Combine soup and stewed tomatoes in saucepan and heat.

- To serve, place dollop of sour cream on top of soup and sprinkle crumbled bacon over sour cream.

*Spicy Sausage Soup

1 pound mild bulk sausage	.5 kg
1 pound hot bulk sausage	.5 kg
2 (15 ounce) cans Mexican stewed tomatoes	2 (425 g)
3 cups chopped celery	710 ml
1 cup sliced carrots	240 ml
1 (15 ounce) can cut green beans, drained	425 g
1 (14 ounce) can chicken broth	396 ml

- Combine mild and hot sausage, shape into small balls and place in non-stick skillet. Brown thoroughly and drain. Place in large slow cooker.

- Add remaining ingredients plus 2 teaspoons (10 ml) salt and 1 cup (240 ml) water and stir gently so meatballs will not break-up. Cover and cook on LOW for 6 to 7 hours.

*Enchilada Soup

1 pound lean ground beef, browned, drained	.5 kg
1 (15 ounce) can Mexican stewed tomatoes	425 g
1 (15 ounce) can pinto beans with liquid	425 g
1 (15 ounce) can whole kernel corn with liquid	425 g
1 onion, chopped	
2 (10 ounce) cans enchilada sauce	2 (280 g)
1 (8 ounce) package shredded 4-cheese blend	1 (227 g)

- Spray 5 to 6-quart (5 to 6 L) slow cooker with cooking spray. Combine beef, tomatoes, beans, corn, onion, enchilada sauce and 1 cup (240 ml) water and mix well.

- Cover and cook on LOW for 6 to 8 hours or on HIGH for 3 to 4 hours. Stir in shredded cheese. If desired, top each serving with a few crushed tortilla chips.

Spaghetti Soup

1 (7 ounce) package pre-cut spaghetti	198 g
1 (18 ounce) package frozen, cooked meatballs, thawed	510 g
1 (28 ounce) jar spaghetti sauce	794 g
1 (15 ounce) can Mexican stewed tomatoes	425 g

- In soup pot or kettle with cook spaghetti about 6 minutes (no need to drain).

- When spaghetti is done, add meatballs, spaghetti sauce and stewed tomatoes and cook until mixture heats.

TIP: To garnish each soup bowl, sprinkle with 2 tablespoons (30 ml) mozzarella cheese or whatever cheese you have in the refrigerator.

*Mexican-Meatball Soup

3 (14 ounce) cans beef broth	3 (396 g)
1 (16 ounce) jar hot salsa	.5 kg
1 (16 ounce) package frozen whole kernel corn, thawed	.5 kg
1 (16 ounce) package frozen meatballs, thawed	.5 kg
1 teaspoon minced garlic	5 ml

- Combine all ingredients in slow cooker and stir well.

- Cover and cook on LOW for 4 to 7 hours.

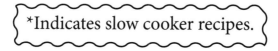

*Indicates slow cooker recipes.

Beefy Vegetable Soup

1 pound lean ground beef	.5 kg
1 (46 ounce) can cocktail vegetable juice	1.3 kg
1 (1 ounce) packet onion soup mix	28 g
1 (3 ounce) package beef-flavored ramen noodles	85 g
1 (16 ounce) package frozen mixed vegetables	.5 kg

- In large soup pot or kettle over medium heat, brown beef and drain. Stir in cocktail juice, soup mix, contents of noodle seasoning packet and mixed vegetables.

- Heat mixture to boiling, reduce heat and simmer uncovered 6 minutes or until vegetables are tender-crisp. Return to boiling, stir in noodles and cook 3 minutes.

Hamburger Soup

2 pound lean ground beef	1 kg
2 (15 ounce) cans chili without beans	2 (425 g)
1 (16 ounce) package frozen mixed vegetables, thawed	454 g
3 (14 ounce) cans beef broth	3 (396 g)
2 (15 ounce) cans stewed tomatoes	2 (425 g)

- In skillet, brown ground beef and place in 6-quart (6 L) slow cooker.

- Add chili, vegetables, broth, tomatoes, 1 cup (240 ml) water and 1 teaspoon (5 ml) salt and stir well. Cover and cook on LOW for 6 to 7 hours.

*Taco Soup

1½ pounds lean ground beef	.7 kg
1 (1 ounce) envelope taco seasoning	28 g
2 (15 ounce) cans Mexican stewed tomatoes	2 (425 g)
2 (15 ounce) cans chili beans with liquid	2 (425 g)
1 (15 ounce) can whole kernel corn, drained	425 g
Crushed tortilla chips	
Shredded cheddar cheese	

- Brown ground beef in skillet and place in 5 to 6-quart (6 L) slow cooker. Add taco seasoning, tomatoes, chili beans and 1 cup (250 ml) water and mix well.

- Cover and cook on LOW for 4 hours or on HIGH for 1 to 2 hours. Serve over crushed tortilla chips and sprinkle some shredded cheddar cheese over top of each serving.

*Taco Soup Olé

2 pounds lean ground beef	1 kg
2 (15 ounce) cans ranch-style beans with liquid	2 (425 g)
1 (15 ounce) can whole kernel corn, drained	425 g
2 (15 ounce) cans stewed tomatoes	2 (425 g)
1 (10 ounce) can tomatoes and green chilies	280 g
1 (1 ounce) package ranch-style dressing mix	28 g
1 (1 ounce) package taco seasoning	28 g

- In large skillet, brown ground beef, drain and transfer to slow cooker.

- Add remaining ingredients and stir well. Cover and cook on LOW for 8 to 10 hours.

TIP: For a nice touch, sprinkle shredded cheddar cheese over each serving.

Meatball Stew

1 (18 ounce) package frozen, cooked	
Italian meatballs	510 g
1 (14 ounce) cans beef broth	396 g
2 (15 ounce) cans Italian stewed tomatoes	2 (425 g)
1 (16 ounce) package frozen stew vegetables	.5 kg

- Place meatballs, beef broth and stewed tomatoes in large saucepan.

- Bring to boiling, reduce heat and simmer for 10 minutes or until meatballs heat through.

- Add vegetables and cook on medium heat for 10 minutes. Mixture will be fairly thin.

- If you like thicker stew, thicken this by mixing 2 tablespoons (30 ml) cornstarch in ¼ cup (60 ml) water and stir into stew, bring to boiling and stir constantly until stew thickens.

**Meatball Stew*

1 (18 ounce) package frozen prepared	
Italian meatballs, thawed	510 g
1 (14 ounce) can beef broth	396 g
1 (15 ounce) can cut green beans, drained	425 g
1 (16 ounce) package baby carrots, drained	.5 kg
2 (15 ounce) cans stewed tomatoes	2 (425 g)
1 tablespoon Worcestershire sauce	15 ml
½ teaspoon ground allspice	2 ml

- Combine all ingredients in slow cooker. Cover and cook on LOW for 3 to 5 hours.

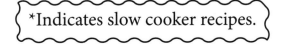

*Indicates slow cooker recipes.

Quick Brunswick Stew

This is great with cornbread!

1 (15 ounce) can beef stew	425 g
1 (15 ounce) can chicken stew	425 g
1 (15 ounce) can lima beans with liquid	425 g
2 (15 ounce) cans stewed tomatoes with liquid	2 (425 g)
1 (15 ounce) can whole kernel corn, drained	425 g
½ teaspoon hot sauce, optional	2 ml

- Combine beef stew, chicken stew, beans, tomatoes and corn in large stew pot. On medium to high heat, bring stew to boil, reduce heat and simmer for 35 minutes.

TIP: *Brunswick stew needs to be a little spicy, so stir in hot sauce. If you don't want the "spicy", add 1 tablespoon (15 ml) Worcestershire sauce to the stew.*

*White Lightning Chili

3 (15 ounce) cans navy beans with liquid	3 (425 g)
3 (14 ounce) cans chicken broth	3 (396 g)
1 (10 ounce) can cream of chicken soup	280 g
2 tablespoons (¼ stick) butter, melted	30 ml
2 onions, chopped	
3 cups cooked, chopped chicken or turkey	710 ml
1 (7 ounce) can chopped green chilies	198 g
1 teaspoon prepared minced garlic	5 ml
½ teaspoon dried basil	2 ml
1 teaspoon ground oregano	5 ml
1 (8 ounce) package shredded 4-cheese blend	227 g

- In slow cooker, combine all ingredients (except cheese) plus ½ teaspoon (2 ml) salt. Cover and cook on LOW for 4 to 5 hours.

- When serving, sprinkle cheese over top of each serving.

*Country Chicken Chowder

1½ pounds boneless, skinless chicken breast halves	.7 kg
2 tablespoons (¼ stick) butter	30 ml
2 (10 ounce) cans cream of potato soup	2 (280 g)
1 (14 ounce) can chicken broth	1 (396 g)
1 (8 ounce) package frozen whole kernel corn	1 (227 g)
1 onion, sliced	
2 ribs celery, sliced	
1 (10 ounce) package frozen peas and carrots, thawed	1 (280 g)
½ teaspoon dried thyme leaves	2 ml
½ cup half-and-half cream	120 ml

- Cut chicken into 1-inch (2.5 cm) strips.

- In skillet, brown chicken strips in butter and transfer to large slow cooker.

- Add soup, broth, corn, onion, celery, peas, carrots and thyme and stir.

- Cover and cook on LOW for 3 to 4 hours or until vegetables are tender.

- Turn off heat, stir in cream and set aside for about 10 minutes before serving.

*Indicates slow cooker recipes.

*Confetti-Chicken Soup

1 pound skinless, boneless chicken thighs	.5 kg
1 (6 ounce) package chicken and herb-flavored rice	168 g
3 (14 ounce) cans chicken broth	3 (396 g)
3 carrots, sliced	
1 (10 ounce) can cream of chicken soup	280 g
1½ tablespoons chicken seasoning	22 ml
1 (10 ounce) package frozen whole kernel corn, thawed	280 g
1 (10 ounce) package frozen baby green peas, thawed	280 g

- Cut thighs in thin strips.

- In 5 or 6-quart (6 L) slow cooker, combine chicken, rice, chicken broth, carrots and 1 cup (240 ml) water.

- Cover and cook on low for 8 to 9 hours.

- About 30 minutes before serving, turn heat to high and add corn and peas to cooker.

- Continue cooking for another 30 minutes.

Chicken-Pasta Soup

1½ pounds boneless, skinless chicken thighs, boned, cubed	.7 kg
1 onion, chopped	
3 carrots, sliced	
½ cup halved pitted ripe olives	120 ml
1 teaspoon prepared minced garlic	5 ml
3 (14 ounce) cans chicken broth	3 (396 g)
1 (15 ounce) can Italian stewed tomatoes	425 g
1 teaspoon Italian seasoning	5 ml
½ cup uncooked small shell pasta	120 ml
Parmesan cheese	

- In slow cooker, combine all ingredients except shell pasta and parmesan cheese.

- Cover and cook on LOW for 8 to 9 hours.

- About 30 minutes before serving, add pasta and stir.

- Increase heat to HIGH and cook another 20 to 30 minutes.

Tasty Turkey Soup

1 (16 ounce) package frozen chopped onions and bell pepper	.5 kg
2 (3 ounce) packages chicken-flavored ramen noodles	2 (84 g)
2 (10 ounce) cans cream of chicken soup	2 (280 g)
1 cup leftover cubed turkey	240 ml

- In soup pot or kettle with a little oil, cook onions and peppers just until tender but not brown. Add ramen noodles, seasoning packet and 2 cups (480 ml) water. Cook 5 minutes or until noodles are tender.

- Stir in chicken soup and cubed turkey. Heat, stirring constantly, until thoroughly hot.

Chicken-Noodle Soup

1 (3 ounce) package chicken-flavored ramen noodles, broken	84 g
1 (10 ounce) package frozen green peas, thawed	280 g
1 (4 ounce) jar sliced mushrooms	114 g
3 cups cooked, cubed chicken or deli turkey	710 g

- In large saucepan, heat 2¼ cups (540 ml) water to boiling and add ramen noodles, contents of seasoning packet and peas. (It's even better if you add 2 tablespoons/30 ml butter.)

- Heat to boiling, reduce heat to medium and cook about 5 minutes. Stir in mushrooms, chicken and ¾ teaspoon (4 ml) black pepper and continue cooking over medium heat until all ingredients heat through

TIP: Garnish with about 1 cup (240 ml) lightly crushed potato chips, if desired.

So Easy Peanut Soup

2 (10 ounce) cans cream of chicken soup	2 (280 g)
2 soups cans milk	
1¼ cups crunchy-style peanut butter	300 ml

- In saucepan on medium heat, blend soup and milk

- Stir in peanut butter and heat until it blends. Serve hot.

*Tasty Chicken and Rice Soup

1 pound boneless skinless chicken breasts	.5 kg
½ cup uncooked brown rice	120 ml
1 (10 ounce) can cream of chicken soup	280 g
1 (10 ounce) can cream of celery soup	280 g
1 (14 ounce) can chicken broth	
with roasted garlic	396 g
1 (16 ounce) package frozen sliced carrots,	
thawed	.5 kg
1 cup half-and-half cream	240 ml

- Cut chicken into 1-inch (2.5 cm) pieces. Place pieces in sprayed 4 or 5-quart (5 L) slow cooker.

- In bowl, mix rice, both soups, chicken broth and carrots and pour over chicken. Cover and cook on LOW 7 to 8 hours.

- Turn heat to HIGH, add half-and-half cream and cook another 15 to 20 minutes.

*Indicates slow cooker recipes.

*Tortellini Soup

1 (1 ounce) package white sauce mix	28 g
3 boneless, skinless chicken breast halves	
1 (14 ounce) can chicken broth	396 g
1 teaspoon minced garlic	5 ml
½ teaspoon dried basil	2 ml
½ teaspoon oregano	2 ml
½ teaspoon cayenne pepper	2 ml
1 (8 ounce) package cheese tortellini	227 g
1½ cups half-and-half cream	360 ml
6 cups fresh baby spinach	1.5 L

- Spray 5 to 6-quart (5 to 6 L) slow cooker with cooking spray and place white sauce mix in cooker.

- Add 4 cups (1 L) water and stir until mixture is smooth. Cut chicken into 1-inch (2.5 cm) pieces.

- Add chicken, broth, garlic, ½ teaspoon (2 ml) salt, basil, oregano and red pepper to mixture.

- Cover and cook on LOW for 6 to 7 hours or on HIGH for 3 hours.

- Stir in tortellini, cover and cook 1 hour more on HIGH. Stir in cream and fresh spinach and cook just enough for soup to get hot.

TIP: Sprinkle a little shredded parmesan cheese on top of each serving as a nice touch.

*Indicates slow cooker recipes.

*Tortilla Soup

3 large boneless, skinless chicken breast halves,
  cubed
1 (10 ounce) package frozen whole kernel corn,
  thawed   280 g
1 onion, chopped
3 (14 ounce) cans chicken broth   3 (396 g)
1 (6 ounce) can tomato paste   168 g
2 (10 ounce) cans tomatoes and green chilies 2 (280 g)
2 teaspoons ground cumin   10 ml
1 teaspoon chili powder   5 ml
1 teaspoon minced garlic   5 ml
6 corn tortillas

- Combine cubed chicken, corn, onion, broth, tomato paste, tomatoes, green chilies, cumin, chili powder, seasoned salt, garlic and 1 teaspoon (5 ml) salt in large slow cooker.

- Cover and cook on LOW for 5 to 7 hours or on HIGH for 3 to 3½ hours.

- While soup is cooking, cut tortillas into ¼-inch (.6 cm) strips and place on baking sheet.

- Bake at 375° (190°) for about 5 minutes or until crisp. Serve baked tortilla strips with soup.

*Indicates slow cooker recipes.

Easy
Big-Time
Beef

Grilled Steak With Garlic-Mustard Sauce

⅓ cup apple juice	80 ml
2 tablespoons dijon-style mustard	30 ml
1 tablespoon minced garlic	15 ml
4 (1-inch) thick boneless beef top strip steaks	2.5 cm

- Combine apple juice, mustard, garlic and 1 teaspoon (5 ml) pepper in bowl and mix well. Remove and reserve ¼ cup (60 ml) sauce for basting. Brush steaks with remaining sauce.

- Grill steaks on grill over medium hot coals. Grill about 15 to 18 minutes or until desired doneness and turn occasionally.

- During last 8 to 10 minutes of grilling, baste steaks with the ¼ cup (60 ml) sauce set aside for basting.

Marinated London Broil

1 (12 ounce) can cola soda	340 g
1 (10 ounce) bottle teriyaki sauce	280 g
1 (3 pound) London broil steak	1.3 kg

- Combine cola, teriyaki sauce and 1 teaspoon (5 ml) pepper in large zip-top freezer bag. Seal, marinate in refrigerator for 24 hours and turn occasionally.

- Remove London broil from marinade and discard marinade. Grill, covered for about 14 minutes on each side.

- Let stand about 10 minutes before slicing diagonally across grain.

*Swiss Steak

1 to 1½ pounds boneless, round steak	.5-.7 kg
8 to 10 medium new (red) potatoes with peels, halved	
1 cup baby carrots	240 ml
1 onion, sliced	
1 (15 ounce) can stewed tomatoes	425 g
1 (12 ounce) jar beef gravy	340 g

- Cut steak in 6 to 8 serving-size pieces, season with ½ teaspoon (2 ml) each of salt and pepper and brown in non-stick skillet.

- Layer steak pieces, potatoes, carrots and onion in slow cooker.

- Combine tomatoes and beef gravy in saucepan and spoon over vegetables. Cover and cook on LOW for 7 to 8 hours.

*Indicates slow cooker recipes.

Steak And Potatoes

2 pounds round steak	1 kg
⅓ cup flour	80 ml
⅓ cup oil	80 ml
5 potatoes, peeled, diced	
¼ cup chopped onions	60 ml
1 (10 ounce) cream of mushroom soup	280 g

- Preheat oven to 350° (176° C). Dice steak and coat in flour and brown in heavy skillet and drain. Place steak in 9-inch (23 cm) baking dish.

- Season potatoes with a little salt and pepper, place over steak and cover with mushroom soup diluted with ½ cup (120 ml) water. Bake 1 hour 30 minutes.

Skillet Steak and Veggies

1 pound boneless sirloin steak, cut in strips	.5 kg
2 (15 ounce) cans Italian stewed tomatoes with juice	2 (425 g)
1 (16 ounce) package frozen Italian green beans, thawed	.5 kg
1 (8 ounce) carton sour cream	227 g

- Place sirloin strips in large skillet with a little oil. Cook on high heat about 3 minutes.

- Add stewed tomatoes and green beans, bring to boiling, lower heat and cook 5 minutes.

- Just before serving, fold in sour cream. Serve over hot, cooked egg noodles.

Zesty Rice and Beef

1 pound lean ground round steak	.5 kg
1 onion, chopped	
1 green bell pepper, chopped	
2½ cups cooked rice	600 ml
1 (15 ounce) whole kernel corn, drained	425 g
1 (15 ounce) can Mexican-style stewed tomatoes	425 g
1 (15 ounce) can diced tomatoes	425 g
2 teaspoons chili powder	10 ml
1 teaspoon garlic powder	5 ml
1 (8 ounce) package cubed processed cheese	227 g
1 cup buttery cracker crumbs	240 ml
½ cup chopped pecans or walnuts	120 ml
2 tablespoons butter, melted	30 ml

- Cook beef, onion and green pepper in large skillet or roaster over medium heat until beef is no longer pink. Drain well.

- Add rice, corn, stewed tomatoes, diced tomatoes, chili powder, garlic powder and 1 teaspoon salt and bring to a boil. Remove from heat.

- Add processed cheese and stir until cheese melts.

- Spoon into greased 9 x 13-inch (23 x 33 cm) baking dish.

- Combine cracker crumbs, pecans and melted butter. Sprinkle over top of casserole. Bake uncovered at 350° (176° C) for 25 minutes or until casserole is bubbly hot.

Thai Beef, Noodles And Veggies

2 (4.4 ounce) packages Thai sesame noodles	2 (120 g)
1 pound sirloin steak, cut in strips	.5 kg
1 (16 ounce) package frozen stir-fry vegetables, thawed	.5 kg
½ cup chopped peanuts	120 ml

- Cook noodles according to package directions, remove from heat and cover.

- Season sirloin strips with a little salt and pepper.

- Brown half sirloin strips in a little oil in skillet and cook about 2 minutes. Remove from skillet and drain.

- Add remaining sirloin strips, brown in skillet with a little oil and cook about 2 minutes.

- In same skillet place vegetables and ½ cup (120 ml) water, cover and cook 5 minutes or until tender-crisp.

- Remove from heat, add steak strips and toss to mix. To serve, sprinkle with chopped peanuts.

On-The-Border Steak

½ teaspoon dry mustard   2 ml
2 tablespoons fajita seasoning   30 ml
1 teaspoon minced garlic   5 ml
1½ pounds flank steak   680 g

- Combine ½ teaspoon (2ml) black pepper, dry mustard, fajita seasoning and garlic. Rub flank steak with a little oil, sprinkle seasonings over steak and chill 4 to 6 hours.

- Grill steak on each side on covered grill 6 to 8 minutes on medium heat. Cut steak diagonally across grain into thin strips.

- Serve with hot salsa over hot cooked rice.

Skillet Sirloin

2 teaspoons minced garlic   10 ml
½ teaspoon cayenne pepper   2 ml
2 tablespoons soy sauce   30 ml
2 tablespoons honey   30 ml
1 pound beef sirloin, thinly sliced   .5 kg

- Combine about 2 teaspoons (10 ml) oil, garlic, cayenne pepper, soy sauce and honey and place in plastic freezer bag.

- Add sliced beef, seal bag and shake. Refrigerate for 30 minutes.

- Place beef mixture in large greased skillet over medium-high heat. Cook 5 to 6 minutes or until desired doneness, but do not over-cook. Serve over hot cooked rice.

Seasoned-Beef Tenderloin

3 tablespoons dijon-style mustard	45 ml
2 tablespoons prepared horseradish	30 ml
1 (3 pound) center-cut beef tenderloin	1.5 kg
½ cup seasoned breadcrumbs	120 ml

- Preheat oven to 375° (190° C). Combine mustard and horseradish and spread over beef tenderloin.

- Spread breadcrumbs into horseradish-mustard mixture and wrap in foil. Refrigerate at least 12 hours.

- Remove wrap and place on greased broiler pan. Bake 30 minutes or to 145° (70° C) for medium rare. Let tenderloin stand for 15 minutes before slicing.

Steak With Creamy Horseradish Sauce

1 (2 pound) sirloin steak	1 kg
1 (8 ounce) carton sour cream	227 g
4 tablespoons prepared, horseradish	60 ml

- Preheat broiler. Pat steak dry and sprinkle liberally with salt and pepper to taste.

- Broil steak on rack about 3 inches (8 cm) from heat for about 5 minutes on both sides. Let stand 5 minutes before slicing.

- Combine sour cream, horseradish and a little salt and pepper and mix well. Serve with sirloin steak.

*Old-Time Pot Roast

1 (2-2½) pound boneless rump roast	1-1.5 kg
5 medium potatoes, peeled, quartered	
1 (16 ounce) package peeled baby carrots	.5 kg
2 medium onions, quartered	
1 (10 ounce) can golden mushroom soup	280 g
½ teaspoon dried basil	2 ml

- In skillet, brown roast on all sides. Place potatoes, carrots and onions in sprayed 4 to 5-quart (5 L) slow cooker.

- Place browned roast on top of vegetables.

- In bowl, combine soup, basil and ½ **teaspoon** (2 ml) salt and pour mixture over meat and vegetables.

- Cover and cook on LOW for 9 to 11 hours.

TIP: To serve, transfer roast and vegetables to serving plate. Stir juices remaining in slow cooker and spoon over roast and vegetables.

*Indicates slow cooker recipes.

*O'Brian's Hash

3 cups cubed, cooked beef roast	710 ml
1 (28 ounce) package frozen hash browns	
with onions and peppers, thawed	794 g
1 (16 ounce) jar salsa	.5 kg
1 tablespoon beef seasoning	15 ml
1 cup shredded cheddar-jack cheese	240 ml

- Place cubed beef in large slow cooker sprayed with vegetable cooking spray.

- Brown potatoes in little oil in large skillet and transfer to slow cooker. Stir in salsa and beef seasoning.

- Cover and cook on HIGH for 4 to 5 hours. When ready to serve, sprinkle cheese over hash.

All-The-Trimmins Corned Beef

1 (4-5 pound) corned beef brisket	1.3-1.8 kg
4 large potatoes, peeled, quartered	
6 carrots, peeled, halved	
4 onions	
1 head cabbage	

- Place corned beef in roasting pan, cover with water and bring to boil. Turn heat down and simmer 3 hours. (Add water if necessary.)

- Add potatoes, carrots and onions, cut cabbage into eighths and lay over top of other vegetables. Bring to boil, turn heat down and cook another 30 to 40 minutes until vegetables are done. When slightly cool, slice corned beef across grain.

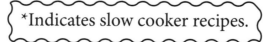

*Indicates slow cooker recipes.

Beef Patties with Mushroom Gravy

1 pound lean ground beef	.5 kg
¼ cup chili sauce	60 ml
1 egg, beaten	
¾ cup crushed cornflakes	180 ml
2 (10 ounce) cans cream of mushroom soup	2 (280 g)

- Combine ground beef, chili sauce, egg, crushed cornflakes and salt and pepper to taste and mix well. Shape into 4 patties, about ¾-inch (1.8 cm) thick.

- Place patties in skillet with a little oil and brown each patty on high heat. Reduce heat, cover and simmer for 10 to 15 minutes.

- Stir in both cans soup with ½ cup (120 ml) water and mix well. Spoon gravy over patties and simmer for about 10 minutes.

TIP: This gravy is great served over mashed potatoes or hot biscuits.

Taco Bueno Bake

2 pounds ground beef	1 kg
1½ cups taco sauce	360 ml
2 (15 ounce) cans Spanish rice	2 (425 g)
1 (8 ounce) package shredded Mexican 4-cheese blend, divided	227 g

• Brown ground beef in skillet and drain. Add taco sauce, rice and half cheese.

• Spoon mixture into buttered 3-quart (3L) baking dish. Cover and bake at 350° (176° C) for 35 minutes.

• Uncover and sprinkle remaining cheese on top and return to oven for 5 minutes.

Skillet Beef and Pasta

1 (8 ounce) package spiral pasta	227 g
1 (14 ounce) can beef broth	396 g
1 pound lean ground beef	.5 kg
2 (11 ounce) cans mexicorn, drained	2 (312 g)
1 (12 ounce) package cubed Mexican processed cheese	340 g

• Cook pasta according to package directions, except for water. Instead of 6 cups water in directions, use 4¼(1.1 L) cups water and 1¾ cups (420 ml) beef broth.

• While pasta cooks, brown beef in large skillet, stir and drain. Stir in corn and cheese and cook on low heat until cheese melts.

• Gently stir cooked pasta into beef mixture until it coats pasta. Spoon mixture into serving bowl and garnish with few springs parsley, if desired.

*Slow-Cook Beef Noodles

1½ pounds lean ground beef	.7 kg
1 (16 ounce) package frozen onions and bell peppers, thawed	.5 kg
1 (16 ounce) box cubed processed cheese	.5 kg
2 (15 ounce) cans Mexican stewed tomatoes with liquid	2 (425 g)
2 (15 ounce) cans whole kernel corn, drained	2 (425 g)
1 (8 ounce) package medium egg noodles	227 g
1 cup shredded cheddar cheese	240 ml

- Brown ground beef in skillet and drain fat.

- Place beef in 5 to 6-quart (5-6 L) slow cooker, add onion, peppers, cheese, tomatoes, corn and about 1 teaspoon (5 ml) salt and mix well. Cover and cook on LOW for 4 to 5 hours.

- Cook noodles according to package direction, drain and fold into beef-tomato mixture.

- Cook another 30 minutes to heat thoroughly.

- When ready to serve, top with cheddar cheese, several sprinkles of chopped fresh parsley or chopped fresh green onions if you like.

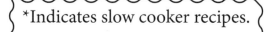

*Indicates slow cooker recipes.

Tex-Mex Supper

1 pound lean ground beef	.5 kg
1 large onion, chopped	
1 (16 ounce) can pinto beans, drained	.5 kg
1½ teaspoons cumin	7 ml
½ head lettuce, torn	
2 tomatoes, chopped	
1 avocado, diced	
3 green onions, chopped	
1 (8 ounce) package shredded cheddar cheese	227 g
1 (10 ounce) bag corn chips, slightly crushed	280 g
Catalina salad dressing	

- Sauté beef and onion in skillet. Drain grease and add beans, spices and 1 cup (240 ml) water and simmer until water cooks out.

- In large serving bowl, combine lettuce, tomatoes, avocado, onions, olives and pimentos.

- When ready to serve, add warm beef mixture, cheese, chips, dressing and toss. Serve immediately. Serves 8.

Simple Casserole Supper

1 pound lean ground beef	.5 kg
¼ cup uncooked white rice	60 ml
1 (10 ounce) can French-onion soup	280 g
1 (6 ounce) can french-fried onion rings	168 g

- Brown ground beef, drain and place in buttered 7 x 11-inch (18 x 28 cm) baking dish. Add rice, onion soup and ½ cup (120 ml) water.

- Cover and bake at 325° (162° C) for 40 minutes. Uncover, sprinkle onion rings over top and return to oven for 10 minutes.

Oriental Beef and Noodles

1¼ pounds ground beef	567 g
2 (3 ounce) packages oriental-flavored ramen noodles	2 (84 g)
1 (16 ounce) package frozen oriental stir-fry mixture	.5 kg
½ teaspoon ground ginger	2 ml
3 tablespoons thinly sliced green onions	45 ml

- Brown ground beef in large skillet and drain. Add ½ cup (120 ml) water, salt and pepper to taste, simmer for 10 minutes and transfer to separate bowl.

- In same skillet, combine 2 cups (480 ml) water, vegetables, noodles (broken up), ginger and both seasoning packets. Bring to boil and reduce heat.

- Cover, simmer 3 minutes or until noodles are tender and stir once. Return beef to skillet and stir in green onions. Serve right from skillet.

Easy Meat 'N Potatoes

1 pound ground beef	.5 kg
1 (10 ounce) can sloppy Joe sauce	280 g
1 (10 ounce) can fiesta nacho cheese soup	280 g
1 (32 ounce) package frozen hash browned potatoes, thawed	1 kg

- Brown beef in skillet over medium heat and drain.

- Add sloppy Joe sauce and fiesta nacho cheese soup to beef and mix well.

- Place hash browns in greased 9 x 13-inch (23 x 33 cm) baking dish and top with beef mixture.

- Cover and bake at 400° (204°) for 25 minutes. Uncover and bake 10 minutes longer.

TIP: *This is really good sprinkled with 1 cup grated cheddar cheese.*

Chili Casserole

1 (40 ounce) can chili with beans	1.1 kg
1 (4 ounce) can chopped green chilies	114 g
1 (2 ounce) can sliced ripe olives, drained	57 g
1 (8 ounce) package shredded cheddar cheese	227 g
2 cups ranch-flavored tortilla chips, crushed	480 ml

- Combine all ingredients and transfer to greased 3-quart (3 L) baking dish.

- Bake uncovered at 350° (176° C) for 35 minutes or until bubbles.

*Cowboy's Tin Plate Supper

1½ pounds lean ground beef	.7 kg
2 onions, coarsely chopped	
5 medium potatoes, peeled, sliced	
1 (15 ounce) can kidney beans, rinsed, drained	425 g
1 (15 ounce) can pinto beans, drained	425 g
1 (15 ounce) can Mexican stewed tomatoes	425 g
1 (10 ounce) can tomato soup	280 g
½ teaspoon basil	2 ml
½ teaspoon oregano	2 ml
2 teaspoons minced garlic	10 ml

- Sprinkle beef with some salt and pepper in skillet, brown meat and drain.

- Place onions in slow cooker and spoon beef over onions.

- On top of beef, layer potatoes, kidney beans and pinto beans.

- Pour stewed tomatoes and tomato soup over beans and potatoes.

- Sprinkle with basil, oregano and garlic. Cover and cook on LOW for 7 to 8 hours.

*Indicates slow cooker recipes.

Ravioli and More

1 pound lean ground beef	.5 kg
1 teaspoon garlic powder	5 ml
1 large onion, chopped	
2 grated zucchini squash	
¼ cup (¼ stick) butter	60 ml
1 (28 ounce) jar spaghetti sauce	794 g
1 (25 ounce) package ravioli with portobello mushrooms, cooked	708 g
1 (12 ounce) package shredded mozzarella cheese	340 g

- Brown ground beef in large skillet until no longer pink and drain. Add garlic powder and ½ teaspoon (2 ml) each of salt and pepper.

- Cook onion and zucchini with butter in saucepan just until tender-crisp and stir in spaghetti sauce. Spread ½ cup (120 ml) sauce in buttered 9 x 13-inch (23 x 33 cm) baking dish.

- Layer half ravioli, half spaghetti sauce, half beef and half cheese. Repeat layers, but save remaining cheese for topping.

- Cover and bake at 350° (176° C) for 35 minutes.

- Uncover and sprinkle remaining cheese on top. Let stand 10 minutes before serving.

Super Spaghetti Pie

*This is a great recipe to make ahead of time and have ready for a
late supper after the game or a midnight supper when teenagers
demand "food"! And, it even resembles pizza.*

1 (8 ounce) package spaghetti	227 g
⅓ cup grated parmesan cheese	80 ml
1 egg, beaten	
1 tablespoon butter, melted	15 ml
1 cup small curd cottage cheese, drained	240 ml
½ pound lean ground beef	227 g
½ pound sausage	227 g
½ cup chopped onion	120 ml
1 (15 ounce) can tomato sauce	425 g
1 teaspoon garlic powder	5 ml
1 tablespoon sugar	15 ml
1 teaspoon oregano	5 ml
½ cup shredded mozzarella cheese	120 ml

- Cook spaghetti according to package directions. While
  spaghetti is still warm, stir in parmesan cheese, egg and
  butter in large bowl.

- Pour into well greased 10-inch (24 cm) pie plate and pat
  mixture up and around sides with spoon to form crust.
  Pour cottage cheese over spaghetti crust.

- In skillet brown ground meat, sausage and onion and
  drain.

- Add tomato sauce, garlic powder, oregano and
  ½ teaspoon (2 ml) each of salt and pepper. Simmer
  10 minutes and stir occasionally.

- Pour meat mixture over cottage cheese. Bake at 350°
  (176° C) for 30 minutes. Arrange mozzarella on top
  and return to oven just until cheese melts.

Company Beef and Pasta

2 pounds lean, ground beef	1 kg
2 onions, chopped	
1 green bell pepper, chopped	
¾ teaspoon garlic powder	4 ml
1 (14 ounce) jar spaghetti sauce	396 g
1 (15 ounce) can Italian stewed tomatoes	425 g
1 (4 ounce) can sliced mushrooms, drained	114 g
1 (8 ounce) package rotini pasta, divided	227 g
1½ pints sour cream, divided	680 g
1 (8 ounce) package sliced provolone cheese	227 g
1 (8 ounce) package shredded mozzarella cheese	227 g

- Brown and cook beef in deep skillet or kettle and stir often to break up pieces. Drain off excess fat.

- Add onions, bell pepper, garlic powder, spaghetti sauce, stewed tomatoes and mushrooms and mix well. Simmer 20 minutes.

- Cook rotini according to package directions and drain. Pour half rotini into buttered deep 11 x 14-inch (30 x 36 cm) baking dish.

- Cover with half meat-tomato mixture and half sour cream. Top with provolone cheese slices. Repeat process once more ending with mozzarella cheese.

- Cover and bake at 350° (176° C) for 35 minutes.

- Remove cover and continue baking another 10 to 15 minutes or until mozzarella cheese melts.

Spaghetti Bake, Etc.

1 (8 ounce) package spaghetti	227 g
1 pound lean ground beef	.5 kg
1 green bell pepper, finely chopped	
1 onion, chopped	
1 (10 ounce) can tomato bisque soup	280 g
1 (15 ounce) can tomato sauce	425 g
2 teaspoons Italian seasoning	10 ml
1 (8 ounce) can whole kernel corn, drained	227 g
1 (4 ounce) can black sliced olives, drained	114 g
1 (12 ounce) package shredded cheddar cheese	340 g

- Cook spaghetti according to package directions, drain and set aside.

- Cook beef, bell pepper, onion in skillet and drain.

- Add remaining ingredients, spaghetti, ⅓ cup water (80 ml) and ½ teaspoon (2 ml) salt to beef mixture and stir well.

- Pour into greased 9 x 13-inch (23 x 33 cm) baking dish and cover.

- Refrigerate 2 to 3 hours and bake covered at 350° (176° C) for 45 minutes.

Enchilada Lasagna

1½ pounds lean ground beef	.7 g
1 onion, chopped	
1 teaspoon minced garlic	5 ml
1 (15 ounce) can enchilada sauce	425 g
1 (15 ounce) can stewed tomatoes	425 g
1 teaspoon cumin	5 ml
1 egg	
1 (12 ounce) carton small curd cottage cheese	340 g
1 (12 ounce) package shredded 4-cheese blend, divided	340 g
8 (8 inch) corn tortillas, torn	8 (20 cm)
1 cup shredded cheddar cheese	240 ml

- Cook beef, onion and garlic in large skillet until meat is no longer pink.

- Stir in enchilada sauce, tomatoes, cumin and ½ teaspoon (2 ml) salt.

- Bring mixture to a boil, reduce heat and simmer uncovered for 20 minutes.

- Combine egg and cottage cheese in small bowl. Spread one-third of meat sauce in greased 9 x 13-inch (23 x 33 cm) baking dish.

- Top with half of 4-cheese blend, tortillas and cottage cheese mixture. Repeat layers.

- Top with remaining meat sauce and sprinkle remaining 1 cup (240 ml) cheddar cheese. Cover and bake at 325° (162° C) for 25 minutes. Uncover and bake 10 more minutes.

Taco Pie

1 pound lean ground beef	.5 kg
½ bell pepper, chopped	
2 jalapeno peppers, seeded, chopped	
1 (15 ounce) can Mexican stewed tomatoes	425 g
1 tablespoon chili powder	15 ml
8 ounces shredded sharp cheddar cheese	227 g
1 (6 ounce) package corn muffin mix	168 g
1 egg	
⅔ cup milk	160 ml

- Brown ground beef, bell pepper and jalapeno peppers in a little oil in large skillet and drain well. Add ½ teaspoon (2 ml) salt, tomatoes, 1 cup (240 ml) water and chili powder. Cook on medium heat for about 10 minutes or until most liquid cooks out, but not dry.

- Pour into greased 9 x 13 inch (23 x 33 cm) glass-baking dish. Sprinkle cheese on top.

- Combine corn muffin mix, egg and milk and beat well. Pour over top of cheese.

- Bake at 375° (190° C) for 25 minutes or until corn muffin mix is light brown.

- Remove from oven and set aside about 10 minutes before serving. Serves 8.

TIP: If you want to make a day ahead, put everything together except corn muffin mixture. Mix corn muffin mix just before you are ready to cook Taco Pie.

Supper's Ready

1 pound lean ground beef	.5 kg
1 onion, chopped	
4 tablespoons steak sauce	60 ml
1 tablespoon flour	15 ml
1 (16 ounce) can baked beans with liquid	454 g
1 (8 ounce) can whole kernel corn, drained	227 g
1½ cups garlic-flavored croutons, crushed	360 ml

- Brown beef and onion in large skillet and drain. Stir in all remaining ingredients except croutons.

- Pour into greased 9 x 13 inch (23 x 33 cm) baking dish. Sprinkle crouton crumbs on top.

- Bake uncovered at 325° (162° C) for 45 minutes or until bubbly around edges. Serves 8.

*TIP: You can make this ahead of time and freeze.
When you need it, just thaw and cook.*

When purchasing ground beef, remember that fat greatly contributes to its flavor. The lower the fat content, the drier it will be once cooked.

Super-Duper Supper

2 pounds lean ground beef	1 kg
1 onion, chopped	
1 (2 pound) package frozen tater tots	1 kg
1 (8 ounce) package shredded cheddar cheese	227 g
2 (10 ounce) cans cream of mushroom soup	2 (280 g)
1 soup can milk	

- Crumble uncooked ground beef into sprayed 9 x 13 inch (23 x 33 cm) glass baking dish. Sprinkle with a little salt and pepper.

- Cover with chopped onion. Top with tater tots and sprinkle cheese.

- Combine soups and milk in saucepan. Heat and stir just enough to mix in milk. Pour over casserole.

- Bake covered at 350° (176° C) for 1 hour. Uncover and bake another 15 minutes.

Cabbage Rolls Along

*This is a wonderful family recipe and a super
way to get the kids to eat cabbage.*

1 large head cabbage, cored	
1½ pounds lean ground beef	.7 kg
1 egg, beaten	
3 tablespoons ketchup	45 ml
⅓ cup seasoned breadcrumbs	80 ml
2 tablespoons dried minced onion flakes	30 ml
2 (15 ounce) cans Italian stewed tomatoes	2 (425 g)
¼ cup cornstarch	60 ml
3 tablespoons brown sugar	45 ml
2 tablespoons Worcestershire sauce	30 ml

- Place head of cabbage in large kettle of boiling water for 10 minutes or until outer leaves are tender. Drain well. Rinse in cold water and remove 10 large outer leaves*. Set aside.

- Slice or grate remaining cabbage. Place in bottom of greased 9 x 13-inch (23 x 33 cm) baking dish. In large bowl combine ground beef, egg, ketchup, breadcrumbs, onion flakes and 1 teaspoon (5 ml) salt and mix well.

- Pack together about ½ cup (120 ml) meat mixture and put on each cabbage leaf. Fold in sides and roll leaf to completely enclose filling*. Place each rolled leaf over grated cabbage.

- Place stewed tomatoes in large saucepan. Combine cornstarch, brown sugar and Worcestershire sauce in bowl and spoon mixture into tomatoes. Cook on high heat, stirring constantly, until stewed tomatoes and juices thicken. Pour over cabbage rolls. Cover and bake at 325° (162° C) for 1 hour.

TIP: To get that many large leaves, you may have to put 2 smaller leaves together to make one roll. Remove the large center vein if leaf is hard to roll.

Chili Relleno Casserole

1 pound lean ground beef	.5 kg
1 bell pepper, chopped	
1 onion, chopped	
1 (4 ounce) can chopped green chilies	114 g
1 teaspoon oregano	5 ml
1 teaspoon dried cilantro leaves	5 ml
¾ teaspoon garlic powder	4 ml
2 (4 ounce) cans whole green chilies	2 (114 g)
1½ cups grated Monterey Jack cheese	360 ml
1½ cups grated sharp cheddar cheese	360 ml
3 large eggs	
1 tablespoon flour	45 ml
1 cup half-and-half cream	240 ml

- Cook meat with bell pepper and onion in skillet.

- Add chopped green chilies, oregano, cilantro, garlic powder and about ½ teaspoon (2 ml) each of salt and pepper.

- Seed whole chilies and spread on bottom of greased 9 x 13-inch (23 x 33 cm) baking dish.

- Cover with meat mixture and sprinkle with cheeses.

- Combine eggs and flour and beat with fork until fluffy.

- Add half-and-half cream, mix and pour slowly over top of meat in casserole.

- Bake uncovered at 350° (176° C) for 35 minutes or until it is light brown.

Enchilada Casserole

1½ pounds lean ground beef	.7 kg
1 (1 ounce) package taco seasoning mix	28 g
Oil	
8 flour or corn tortillas	
1 cup shredded cheddar cheese	240 ml
1 onion, chopped	
1 (10 ounce) can enchilada sauce	280 g
1 (7 ounce) can green chilies	198 g
1½ cups grated Monterey Jack cheese	360 ml
1 (8 ounce) carton sour cream	227 g

- Brown beef in skillet with a little salt and pepper until it crumbles and is brown. Drain well.

- Add taco seasoning mix and 1¼ cups (300 ml) water to beef and simmer 5 minutes.

- In another skillet pour just enough oil to cover bottom of skillet and heat until oil is hot.

- Cook tortillas one at a time, until soft and limp, about 5 to 10 seconds on each side. Drain on paper towels.

- As you cook tortillas, spoon ⅓ cup (80 ml) meat mixture into center of each tortilla. Sprinkle with small amount of cheddar cheese and 1 spoonful of chopped onion. Roll up and place seam-side down in greased 9 x 13-inch (23 x 33 cm) baking dish.

- After filling all tortillas, add enchilada sauce and green chilies to remaining meat mixture. Spoon over tortillas. Cover and bake at 350° (176° C) for about 30 minutes.

- Uncover and sprinkle remaining cheddar cheese and Monterey Jack cheese over casserole.

- Return to oven just until cheese melts. Place dabs of sour cream over enchiladas to serve.

Spiced Beef

1 pound lean ground beef	.5 kg
1 (1 ounce) package taco seasoning mix	28 g
1 (16 ounce) can Mexican-style stewed tomatoes	
with liquid	.5 kg
1 (16 ounce) can kidney beans with liquid	.5 kg
1 (1 pound) package egg noodles	.5 kg

- Cook beef in skillet and drain. Add taco seasoning and ½ cup (120 ml) water and simmer 15 minutes.

- Add stewed tomatoes and kidney beans. (You may need to add ¼ teaspoon (1 ml) salt.

- Cook egg noodles according to package directions and serve beef over noodles.

Shepherds' Pie

1 pound lean ground beef	.5 kg
1 (1 ounce) envelope taco seasoning mix	28 g
1 cup shredded cheddar cheese	240 ml
1 (11 ounce) can whole kernel corn, drained	312 g
2 cups instant cooked, mashed potatoes	480 ml

- In skillet, brown beef, cook 10 minutes and drain. Add taco seasoning and ¾ cup (180 ml) water and cook another 5 minutes.

- Spoon beef mixture into 8-inch (20 cm) baking pan and sprinkle cheese on top.

- Sprinkle with corn and spread mashed potatoes over top. Bake at 350° (176° C) for 25 minutes or until top is golden.

Quick Skillet

1½ pounds lean ground beef	.7 kg
⅔ cup stir-fry sauce	160 ml
1 (16 ounce) package frozen stir-fry vegetables	.5 kg
2 (3 ounce) packages Oriental-flavor ramen noodles	2 (84 g)

- Brown and crumble ground beef in large skillet. Add 2½ cups (600 ml) water, stir-fry sauce to taste, vegetables and seasoning packets with ramen noodles.

- Cook and stir on low to medium heat about 5 minutes.

- Break noodles, add to beef-vegetable mixture and cook about 6 minutes. Stir to separate noodles as they soften.

Potato-Beef Casserole

4 medium potatoes, peeled, sliced	
1¼ pounds lean ground beef, browned, drained	567 g
1 (10 ounce) can cream of mushroom soup	280 g
1 (10 ounce) can condensed vegetable beef soup	280 g

- In large bowl, combine all ingredients. Add a little salt and pepper to taste. Transfer to greased 3-quart (3 L) baking dish.

- Bake covered at 350° (176° C) for 1 hour 30 minutes or until potatoes are tender.

Pinto Bean Pie

1 pound lean ground beef	.5 kg
1 onion, chopped	
2 (16 ounce) cans pinto beans with liquid	2 (.5 kg)
1 (10 ounce) can tomatoes and green chilies with liquid	280 g
1 (6 ounce) can french-fried onion rings	168 g

- In skillet, brown beef and onion and drain. In 2-quart (2 L) casserole dish, layer 1 can beans, beef-onion mixture and ½ can tomatoes and green chilies and repeat layer.

- Top with onion rings and bake uncovered at 350° (176° C) for 30 minutes.

Beef Picante Skillet

This is a good family dish! And you can take the skillet right to the table.

1 pound lean ground beef	.5 kg
1 (10 ounce) can tomato soup	280 g
1 cup chunky salsa	240 ml
6 (6 inch) flour tortillas, cut into 1-inch pieces	6 (15 cm)
1¼ cups shredded cheddar cheese	300 ml

- Cook beef in skillet until brown and drain.

- Add soup, salsa, ¾ cup (180 ml) water, tortillas, ½ teaspoon (2 ml) salt and half the cheese. Heat to boil. Cover and cook over low heat 5 minutes.

- Top with remaining cheese. Serve right from skillet.

Chili-Relleno Fiesta

1 pound lean ground beef	.5 kg
1 bell pepper, chopped	
1 onion, chopped	
1 (4 ounce) can chopped green chilies, drained	114 g
1 teaspoon oregano	5 ml
1 teaspoon dried cilantro leaves	5 ml
½ teaspoon garlic powder	2 ml
1 (7 ounce) can whole green chilies, drained	198 g
1½ cups grated Monterey Jack cheese	360 ml
1½ cups sharp cheddar cheese	360 ml
3 large eggs	
1 tablespoon flour	15 ml
1 cup half-and-half cream	240 ml

- Preheat oven to 350° (176° C). Brown meat with bell pepper, onion, chopped green chilies, oregano, cilantro, garlic powder and ½ teaspoon (2 ml) each of salt and pepper.

- Seed whole chili peppers and spread on bottom of sprayed 9 x 13-inch (23 x 33 cm) baking dish.

- Cover with meat mixture and sprinkle with cheeses. Combine eggs and flour and beat with fork until fluffy.

- Add half-and-half cream, mix well and pour over top of meat in baking dish. Bake for 30 to 35 minutes or until light brown.

TIP: You could use chopped green chilies instead of the whole green chilies.

Reuben Dogs

1 (27 ounce) can sauerkraut, rinsed, drained   780 g
2 teaspoons caraway seeds   10 ml
8 all-beef wieners, halved lengthwise
1 cup shredded Swiss cheese   240 ml
Thousand Island salad dressing

- Place sauerkraut in greased 2-quart (2 L) baking dish. Sprinkle caraway seeds over top and add wieners.

- Bake uncovered at 350° (176° C) for 20 minutes or until they are hot. Sprinkle with cheese. Bake 3 to 5 minutes longer or until cheese melts. Serve with salad dressing.

Reuben Casserole

1 (20 ounce) package frozen hash brown potatoes,
   thawed   567 g
2 pounds deli corned beef, sliced ¼-inch thick   1 kg
1 (15 ounce) can sauerkraut, drained   425 g
8 slices Swiss cheese
1 (8 ounce) bottle Russian salad dressing,
   divided   227 g

- Preheat oven to 425° (220° C). Place hash brown potatoes in greased 9 x 13-inch (23 x 33 cm) baking dish and season with a little salt and pepper. Bake uncovered for 25 minutes.

- Place overlapping corned beef slices on top of potatoes. Spoon half bottle of dressing over top of beef and arrange sauerkraut over beef. Cover with slices of cheese.

- Reduce oven to 375° (190° C) and bake for 20 minutes. Serve remaining Russian dressing on the side.

Corned Beef Supper

4-5 pound corned beef brisket   1.8 kg
4 large potatoes, peeled, quartered
6 carrots, peeled, halved
1 head cabbage

- Place corned beef in roaster and cover with water. Bring to boil. Turn heat down and simmer 3 hours. Add water if necessary.

- Add potatoes and carrots on and around brisket. Cut cabbage into eighths and lay over top of potatoes, carrots and brisket.

- Bring to a boil, turn heat down and cook another 30 to 40 minutes or until vegetables are tender. Slice corned beef across the grain.

TIP: Leftover corned beef is great on sandwiches.

Remember that limp vegetables like carrots and potatoes regain much of their crispness if soaked in ice water for at least 1 hour.

Quick-Friday-Night-Game Supper

2 (15 ounce) cans chili without beans	2 (425 g)
2 (15 ounce) cans pinto beans with liquid	2 (425 g)
2 (15 ounce) cans beef tamales without shucks	2 (425 g)
1 (8 ounce) package shredded Mexican 4-cheese blend, divided	227 g

- Preheat oven to 350° (176° C).

- In greased 9 x 13-inch (23 x 33 cm) baking pan, spoon both cans chili in pan and spread out with back of large spoon.

- Spread beans with liquid over chili. Spread tamales over beans. Sprinkle about ½ cup (120 ml) cheese over top, cover and bake 30 minutes.

- Remove from oven and sprinkle remaining cheese over top of casserole.

- Return to oven for just 5 minutes. Serve with lots of tortilla chips.

> TIP: You might want to serve some hot thick, chunky salsa
> along with this dish.

Corny Chili and Beans

2 (15 ounce) cans chili with beans	2 (425 g)
1 (15 ounce) can Mexican style stewed tomatoes	425 g
1 (11 ounce) can Mexicorn, drained	312 g
2 diced ripe avocados	

- Combine chili, tomatoes and corn in microwave-safe bowl. Cover loosely and cook on high in microwave for about 4 minutes.

- Stir in diced avocados and serve hot.

Extra Special Queso

1 pound lean ground beef	.5 kg
1 (15 ounce) jar medium salsa con queso	425 g
1 (16 ounce) jar salsa	.5 kg
1 (15 ounce) can black beans, rinsed, drained	425 g

- Cook meat over medium heat in skillet and stir in queso, salsa and black beans.

- Bring mixture to boil and stir constantly. Reduce heat to low and simmer for 5 minutes.

- Serve with tortilla scoops.

Easy
Crunchy
Chicken

*Tasty Chicken-Rice and Veggies

4 boneless, skinless chicken breast halves
2 (10 ounce) jars sweet-and-sour sauce   2 (280 g)
1 (16 ounce) package frozen broccoli, cauliflower
   and carrots, thawed   .5 g
1 (10 ounce) package frozen baby peas, thawed   280 g
2 cups sliced celery   480 ml
1 (6 ounce) package parmesan-butter rice mix   168 g
⅓ cup slivered almonds, toasted   80 ml

- Cut chicken in 1-inch (2.5 cm) strips.

- Combine chicken, sweet-and-sour sauce and all vegetables in 6-quart (6 L) slow cooker sprayed with vegetable cooking spray.

- Cover and cook on LOW for 4 to 6 hours.

- When ready to serve cook parmesan-butter rice according to package directions and fold in almonds.

- Serve chicken and vegetables over hot cooked rice.

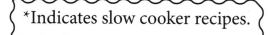

*Indicates slow cooker recipes.

*Golden Chicken Dinner

6 medium new potatoes with peels, cubed
6 medium carrots
5 boneless, skinless chicken breast halves
1 tablespoon dried parsley flakes   15 ml
1 (10 ounce) can golden mushroom soup   280 g
1 (10 ounce) can cream of chicken soup   280 g
4 tablespoons dried mashed potato flakes   60 ml

- Cut chicken into ½-inch (1.2 cm) pieces.

- Place potatoes and carrots in slow cooker and top with chicken breasts. Sprinkle parsley flakes, 1 teaspoon (5 ml) salt and a little pepper over chicken.

- Combine soups and spread over chicken. Cover and slow cook on LOW for 6 to 7 hours.

- Stir in potato flakes and a little water or milk if necessary to make gravy and cook another 30 minutes.

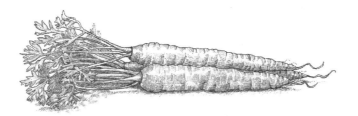

*Indicates slow cooker recipes.

Tortellini Supper

1 (9 ounce) package refrigerated cheese tortellini	255 g
1 (10 ounce) package frozen green peas, thawed	280 g
1 (8 ounce) carton cream cheese with chives and onion	227 g
½ cup sour cream	120 ml
1 (9 ounce) package frozen cooked chicken breasts	255 g

- Cook cheese tortellini in saucepan according to package directions.

- Place peas in colander and pour hot pasta water over green peas. Return tortellini and peas to saucepan.

- Combine cream cheese and sour cream in smaller saucepan and heat on low, stirring well, until cheese melts.

- Spoon mixture over tortellini and peas and toss with heat on low.

- Heat cooked chicken in microwave according to package directions.

- Spoon tortellini and peas in serving bowl and place chicken on top. Serve hot.

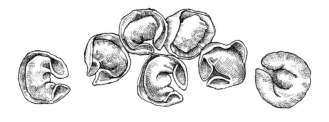

*Indicates slow cooker recipes.

*Delightful Chicken and Veggies

4 to 5 boneless skinless, chicken breast halves
1 (15 ounce) can whole kernel corn, drained   425 g
1 (10 ounce) box frozen green peas, thawed   280 g
1 (16 ounce) jar alfredo sauce   .5 g
1 teaspoon chicken seasoning   5 ml
1 teaspoon prepared minced garlic   5 ml

- Brown chicken breasts in skillet and place in oval slow cooker sprayed with vegetable cooking spray.

- Combine corn, peas, alfredo sauce, ¼ cup (60 ml) water, chicken seasoning and minced garlic and pour over chicken breasts. Cover and cook on LOW for 4 to 5 hours. Serve over hot cooked pasta.

*Chicken-Supper Ready

6 medium new potatoes with peels, quartered
4 to 5 carrots
4 to 5 boneless, skinless chicken breast halves
1 tablespoon chicken seasoning   15 ml
2 (10 ounce) cans cream of chicken soup   2 (280 g)
⅓ cup white wine or cooking wine   80 ml

- Cut carrots into ½-inch pieces. Place potatoes and carrots in slow cooker. Sprinkle chicken breasts with chicken seasoning and place over vegetables.

- Spoon soups mixed with ¼ cup (60 ml) water over chicken and vegetables. Cover and cook on LOW for 5 to 6 hours.

TIP: For a tasty change, use 1 (10 ounce/280 g) can chicken soup and 1 (10 ounce/280 g) can mushroom soup instead of cream of chicken soup.

Chicken-Orzo Florentine

4 boneless, skinless chicken breast halves	
¾ cup uncooked orzo	180 ml
1 (8 ounce) package fresh mushrooms, sliced	227 g
1 (10 ounce) package frozen spinach, thawed, well drained	280 g
1 (10 ounce) can golden mushroom soup	280 g
½ cup mayonnaise	120 ml
1 tablespoon lemon juice	15 ml
1 (8 ounce) package shredded Monterey Jack cheese	227 g
½ cup seasoned Italian breadcrumbs	120 ml

- Cook chicken in boiling water for about 15 minutes and reserve broth. Cut chicken in bite-size pieces and set aside.

- Pour broth through strainer and cook orzo in remaining broth.

- Saute mushrooms in large, sprayed skillet until tender.

- Remove from heat and stir in chicken, orzo, spinach, soup, mayonnaise, lemon juice and ½ teaspoon (2 ml) pepper. Fold in 4 ounces (114 g) cheese and mix well.

- Spoon into greased 9 x 13-inch (23 x 33 cm) baking dish and sprinkle with remaining cheese and breadcrumbs.

- Bake uncovered at 350° (176° C) for 35 minutes.

Lemon-Almond Chicken

Asparagus, lemon juice, curry powder and almonds give a flavorful twist to an otherwise ordinary chicken dish.

2 (14 ounce) cans cut asparagus, well drained	2 (396 g)
4 boneless, skinless chicken breast halves, cut into ½-inch (1.2 cm) strips	
3 tablespoons butter	45 ml
1 (10 ounce) can cream of asparagus soup	280 g
⅔ cup mayonnaise	160 ml
¼ cup milk	60 ml
1 sweet red bell pepper, cut in strips	
2 tablespoons lemon juice	30 ml
1 teaspoon curry powder	5 ml
¼ teaspoon ground ginger	1 ml
½ cup sliced almonds, toasted	120 ml

- Place asparagus in buttered 7 x 11-inch (18 x 28 cm) baking dish and set aside. Sprinkle chicken with salt and pepper.

- In large skillet, saute chicken in butter for about 15 minutes.

- Spoon chicken strips over asparagus.

- In skillet, combine asparagus soup, mayonnaise, milk, red bell pepper, lemon juice, curry powder, ginger and ½ teaspoon (2 ml) salt and ¼ teaspoon (1 ml) pepper and heat just enough to mix well.

- Spoon over chicken and sprinkle almonds over top of casserole.

- Bake uncovered at 350° (176° C) for 35 minutes.

Italian Chicken Over Polenta

1 pound frozen chicken tenders, each cut in half .5 kg
1 onion, chopped
1 (15 ounce) can Italian stewed tomatoes   425 g
⅔ cup pitted kalamata olives   160 ml

- Season chicken with a little salt and pepper. Place in large skillet with a little oil.

- Over medium to high heat add onion, cook about 8 minutes, covered, and turn once.

- Add tomatoes and olives, cover and cook another 8 minutes or until chicken is done.

Polenta:
¾ cup cornmeal   180 ml
⅔ cup grated parmesan cheese   160 ml

- For polenta, place 2½ cups (600 ml) water in saucepan and bring to boiling.

- Stir in cornmeal and ½ teaspoon (2 ml) salt and cook, stirring occasionally, until mixture starts to thicken.

- Stir in cheese. Spoon polenta onto serving plates and top with chicken and sauce.

Spicy Orange Chicken
Over Noodles

1 pound boneless, skinless chicken tenders	.5 kg
2 tablespoons oil	30 ml
2 tablespoons soy sauce	30 ml
1 (16 ounce) package frozen stir-fry vegetables, thawed	.5 g

- Lightly brown chicken tenders in oil in large skillet over medium to high heat.

- Add 2 tablespoons (30 ml) soy sauce and cook another 3 minutes.

- Add stir-fry vegetables and cook about 5 minutes or until vegetables are tender-crisp.

Sauce:

⅔ cup orange marmalade	160 ml
1 tablespoon oil	15 ml
1 tablespoon soy sauce	15 ml
1½ teaspoons lime juice	7 ml
½ teaspoon minced ginger	2 ml
½ teaspoon cayenne pepper	2 ml

- In saucepan, combine marmalade, oil, soy sauce, lime juice, minced ginger and cayenne pepper and mix well.

- Heat and pour over stir-fry chicken and vegetables. Serve over chow mein noodles.

Honey-Glazed Chicken

4 skinless, boneless chicken breast halves
½ cup refrigerated dijon-style honey mustard   120 ml
1 green and 1 red bell pepper, thinly sliced
1 (20 ounce) can pineapple chunks with juice   567 g

- Cut chicken breasts into strips, add a little salt and pepper and brown in large skillet with a little oil.

- Add juice from pineapple, cover and simmer for 15 minutes.

- Add honey mustard, pepper slices and pineapple chunks to chicken. Bring to boil, reduce heat, cover and simmer for another 15 minutes. Serve over hot, cooked couscous.

Summertime-Limeade Chicken

6 large boneless, skinless chicken breast halves
1 (6 ounce) can frozen limeade concentrate,
    thawed   168 g
3 tablespoons brown sugar   45 ml
½ cup chili sauce   120 ml

- Sprinkle chicken breasts with a little salt and pepper and place in lightly greased skillet. Cook on high heat and brown on both sides for about 10 minutes. Remove from skillet, but set aside and keep warm.

- Add limeade concentrate, brown sugar and chili sauce to skillet. Bring to boil and cook, stirring constantly, for 4 minutes.

- Return chicken to skillet and spoon sauce over chicken. Reduce heat, cover and simmer for 15 minutes. Serve over hot, buttered rice.

Three Cheers for Chicken

This chicken casserole is a meal in itself. Just add a tossed green salad and you have a completely, delicious, satisfying meal.

8 boneless, skinless chicken breast halves	
6 tablespoons (¾ stick) butter	90 ml
1 cup chopped celery	240 ml
1 onion, chopped	
1 small bell pepper, chopped	
1 (4 ounce) jar chopped pimentos, drained	114 g
1 cup uncooked rice	240 ml
1 (10 ounce) can cream of chicken soup	280 g
1 (10 ounce) can cream of celery soup	280 g
2 soup cans milk	
1 (8 ounce) can sliced water chestnuts, drained	227 g
1½ cups shredded cheddar cheese	360 ml

- Place chicken breasts in large, greased 11 x 14-inch (28 x 36 cm) baking dish and sprinkle with a little seasoned salt and pepper.

- Melt butter in large skillet and saute celery, onion and bell pepper.

- Add pimentos, rice, soups, milk and water chestnuts and mix well. Pour mixture over chicken breasts.

- Cook chicken covered at 325° (162° C) for 1 hour.

- Uncover and cook another 10 minutes. Remove from oven, sprinkle cheese over top of casserole and bake 5 minutes longer.

*Creamed Chicken and Vegetables

4 large boneless, skinless chicken breast halves	
1 (10 ounce) can cream of chicken soup	280 g
1 (16 ounce) package frozen peas and carrots,	
thawed	.5 g
1 (12 ounce) jar chicken gravy	340 g

- Cut chicken in thin slices. Spray 6-quart (6 L) slow cooker with vegetable cooking spray.

- Pour soup and ½ cup (120 ml) water into slow cooker, mix and add chicken slices.

- Sprinkle a little salt and lots of pepper over chicken and soup. Cover and cook on LOW for 4 to 5 hours.

- Add peas, carrots, chicken gravy and another ½ cup (120 ml) water. Increase heat to HIGH and cook for about 1 hour or until peas and carrots are tender.

TIP: Serve over large, refrigerated buttermilk biscuits or over thick, Texas toast.

*Indicates slow cooker recipes.

Chicken-Tortilla Dumplings

These dumplings are wonderful. This recipe is actually easy. It just takes a little time to add tortilla strips, one at a time but it is certainly a lot easier than making up biscuit dough for dumplings!

6 large boneless, skinless chicken breasts	
2 celery ribs, chopped	
1 onion, chopped	
2 tablespoons chicken bouillon	30 ml
1 (10 ounce) can cream of chicken soup	280 g
10-11 (8 inch) flour tortillas	18 cm

- Place chicken breasts, 10 cups (2.2 L) water, celery and onion in very large kettle or roasting pan.

- Bring to boil, reduce heat and cook about 30 minutes or until chicken is tender. Remove chicken and set aside to cool.

- Save broth in roasting pan. (You should have about 9 cups/2 L broth.) Add chicken bouillon and taste to make sure it is rich and flavorful. (Add more bouillon if needed and more water if you don't have 9 cups/2 L of broth.)

- When chicken is cool enough, cut into bite-size pieces and set aside. Add chicken soup to broth and bring to boil.

- Cut tortillas into 2 x 1-inch (5 x 2.5 cm) strips. Add strips, one at a time, to briskly boiling broth mixture and stir constantly.

- When all strips are in saucepan, pour in chicken, reduce heat to low, simmer 5 to 10 minutes and stir well but gently, to prevent dumplings from sticking.

TIP: Your kettle of chicken and dumplings will be very thick. Pour into very large serving bowl and serve hot.

Sunny Chicken Supper

1½ teaspoons curry powder	7 ml
4 boneless, skinless chicken breast halves	
1½ cups orange juice	360 ml
1 tablespoon brown sugar	15 ml
1 cup uncooked rice	240 ml
1 teaspoon mustard	5 ml

- Rub chicken breasts with curry powder and a little salt and pepper. Combine orange juice, brown sugar, rice and mustard in large skillet and mix well.

- Place chicken breasts on top of rice mixture and bring to boil. Reduce heat, cover and simmer for 30 minutes.

- Remove from heat and let stand, covered, about 10 minutes until all liquid absorbs into rice.

Stir-Fry Cashew Chicken

1 pound chicken tenders, cut into strips	.5 kg
1 (16 ounce) package frozen broccoli, cauliflower and carrots	.5 kg
1 (8 ounce) jar stir-fry sauce	227 g
⅓ cup cashew halves	80 ml
1 (12 ounce) package chow mein noodles	340 g

- Place a little oil and stir-fry chicken strips in 12-inch (32 cm) wok or skillet over high heat for about 4 minutes.

- Add vegetables and stir-fry another 4 minutes or until vegetables are tender.

- Stir in stir-fry sauce and cook just until mixture is hot. Serve over chow mein noodles.

Stir-Fry Chicken Spaghetti

1 pound boneless, skinless chicken breast halves	.5 kg
1½ cups sliced mushrooms	360 ml
1½ cups bell pepper strips	360 ml
1 cup sweet-and-sour stir-fry sauce	240 ml
1 (16 ounce) package spaghetti, cooked	.5 kg
¼ cup (½ stick) butter	60 ml

- Season chicken with salt and pepper and cut into thin slices.

- Brown chicken slices in large skillet with a little oil and cook for 5 minutes on low to medium heat. Transfer to plate and set aside.

- In same skillet with a little more oil, stir-fry mushrooms and bell pepper strips for 5 minutes.

- Add chicken strips and sweet and sour sauce and stir until ingredients are hot.

- While spaghetti is still hot, drain well, add butter and stir until butter melts.

- Place in large bowl and toss with chicken mixture. Serve hot.

Skillet Chicken and Peas

4-5 boneless, skinless chicken breast halves
2 (10 ounce) can cream of chicken soup   2 (280 g)
2 cups uncooked instant rice   480 ml
1 (10 ounce) package frozen green peas   280 g

- Heat a little oil in very large skillet. Add chicken and cook until it browns well. Transfer chicken to plate and keep warm.

- To skillet, add soup, 1¾ cups (420 ml) water and about ½ teaspoon (2 ml) pepper and paprika if you have it.

- Heat to boiling, stir in rice and peas and reduce heat. Place chicken on top and cook on low heat for 15 minutes.

Skillet Chicken and More

4 boneless, skinless chicken breast halves
2 (10 ounce) cans cream of chicken soup   2 (280 g)
2 cups uncooked, instant white rice   480 ml
1 (16 ounce) package broccoli florets   .5 kg

- Brown chicken breasts on both sides in very large skillet with a little oil and simmer 10 minutes.

- Remove chicken and keep warm. Add soup and 2 cups (480 ml) water. Heat to boiling.

- Stir in instant rice and broccoli florets. Use a little salt, pepper and paprika (if you have it) on chicken and place on top of rice.

- Cover dish and cook on low 15 minutes or until liquid evaporates.

Sassy Chicken over Tex-Mex Corn

2 teaspoons garlic powder	10 ml
1 teaspoon ground cumin	5 ml
⅔ cup flour	160 ml
4 boneless, skinless chicken breast halves	

Tex Mex Corn:

1 (10 ounce) can chicken broth	280 g
1½ cups hot salsa	360 ml
1 (11 ounce) can mexicorn	312 g
1 cup instant rice	240 ml

- Combine garlic powder, cumin, flour and ample salt in shallow bowl.

- Dip chicken in flour mixture and coat each side of chicken.

- Place a little oil in heavy skillet over medium to high heat. Cut each chicken breast in half lengthwise.

- Brown each piece of chicken on both sides, reduce heat and add 2 tablespoons (30 ml) water to skillet.

- Cover and simmer for 15 minutes. Transfer chicken to foil-lined baking pan and place in oven at 250° (121° C) until Tex-Mex Corn is ready to serve.

- Use same unwashed skillet, combine broth, salsa and corn and cook about 10 minutes. Stir in rice and let stand 10 minutes or until rice is tender.

- To serve, spoon Tex-Mex Corn on platter and place chicken breasts over corn.

Roasted Chicken and Vegetables

3 pounds chicken pieces	1.3 kg
1 cup lemon pepper marinade with lemon juice, divided	240 ml
1 (16 ounce) package frozen mixed vegetables, thawed	.5 kg
¼ cup olive oil	60 ml

- Spray baking pan with non-stick vegetable spray.

- Arrange chicken skin-side down in pan. Pour ⅔ cup (160 ml) marinade over chicken.

- Bake uncovered at 375° (190° C) for 30 minutes.

- Turn chicken over and baste with remaining ⅓ cup (80 ml) marinade.

- Toss vegetables with oil and 1 teaspoon (5 ml) salt.

- Arrange vegetables around chicken and cover with foil. Return pan to oven and bake another 30 minutes.

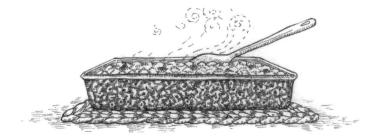

Chicken Bake Baby

1 (1 ounce) package vegetable soup-dip mix	28 g
1 (6 ounce) package chicken stuffing mix	168 g
4 boneless, skinless chicken breast halves	
1 (10 ounce) can cream of mushroom soup	280 g
⅓ cup sour cream	80 ml

- Toss contents of vegetable-seasoning packet, stuffing mix and 1⅔ cups (400 ml) water and set aside.

- Place chicken in greased 9 x 13-inch (23 x 33 cm) baking dish.

- Mix soup and sour cream in saucepan over low heat just enough to pour over chicken.

- Spoon stuffing evenly over top. Bake uncovered at 375° (190° C) for 40 minutes.

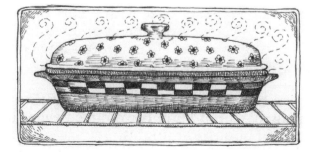

Chicken Super Supper

5 boneless, skinless chicken breast halves
5 slices onion
5 potatoes, peeled, quartered
1(10 ounce) can cream of celery soup   280 g

- Place chicken breasts in 9 x 13-inch (23 x 33 cm) greased baking dish. Top chicken with onion slices and place potatoes around chicken.

- Heat soup with ¼ cup (60 ml) water just enough to pour soup over chicken and vegetables. Bake covered at 325° (162° C) for 1 hour 10 minutes.

Chicken Cacciatore

Chicken:
1 (2½ pound) frying chicken   1.1 kg
2 onions, sliced

Sauce:
1 (15 ounce) can stewed tomatoes   425 g
1 (8 ounce) can tomato sauce   227 g
1 teaspoon dried oregano   5 ml
1 teaspoon celery seed   5 ml

- Quarter chicken and sprinkle with plenty of salt and black pepper. Place in large skillet on medium to high heat with a little oil. Add sliced onions and cook until chicken is tender, about 15 minutes.

- Add stewed tomatoes, tomato sauce, oregano and celery seed. Bring mixture to boiling, reduce heat and simmer uncovered for about 20 minutes.

TIP: This is great over hot cooked noodles or spaghetti.

Chicken and the Works

6 boneless, skinless chicken breast halves
2 (10 ounce) cans cream of chicken soup   2 (280 g)
2 cups uncooked, instant white rice   480 ml
1 (10 ounce) package frozen green peas, thawed   280 g

- Sprinkle chicken with pepper and paprika and brown in large, 12-inch (32 cm) skillet with a little oil. Reduce heat, cover and simmer about 15 minutes. Transfer chicken to plate and keep warm.

- Add soup, 2 cups (480 ml) water and mix well. Heat to boiling and stir in rice and green peas. Top with chicken breasts, cover and simmer over low heat about 10 minutes.

Chicken and Sauerkraut

6 large, boneless, skinless chicken breast halves
1 (16 ounce) can sliced potatoes, drained   .5 g
1 (16 ounce) can sauerkraut, drained   .5 g
¼ cup pine nuts or ½ teaspoon caraway seeds   60 ml; 2 ml

- Season chicken in prepared large skillet with a little pepper and cook over medium heat for 15 minutes or until chicken browns on both sides.

- Add potatoes to skillet and spoon sauerkraut over potatoes. Cover and cook over low heat for 35 minutes or until chicken is done.

- Toast pine nuts in dry skillet on medium heat until golden brown. Stir constantly. Sprinkle chicken and sauerkraut with toasted pine nuts or caraway seeds and serve.

TIP: This is good served with sour cream.

Broccoli-Cheese Chicken

1 tablespoon butter	15 ml
4 boneless, skinless chicken breast halves	
1 (10 ounce) can condensed broccoli-cheese soup	280 g
1 (10 ounce) package frozen broccoli spears	280 g
⅓ cup milk	80 ml

- Heat butter in skillet, cook chicken 15 minutes or until brown on both sides, remove and set aside.

- In same skillet, combine soup, broccoli, milk and a little black pepper and heat to boiling, return chicken to skillet and reduce heat to low.

- Cover and cook another 25 minutes until chicken is no longer pink and broccoli is tender and serve over rice.

Jambalaya

1 (8 ounce) package jambalaya mix	227 g
1 (6 ounce) package frozen chicken breast strips, thawed	168 g
1 (11 ounce) can mexicorn, drained	312 g
1 (2 ounce) can chopped black olives	57 g

- Combine jambalaya mix and 2¼ cups (540 ml) water in soup or large saucepan. Heat to boiling, reduce heat and cook slowly 5 minutes.

- Add chopped chicken, corn and black olives. Heat to boiling, reduce heat and simmer about 20 minutes.

    TIP: You could also add leftover ham or sausage and 1 tablespoon (15 ml) lemon juice to change it up some.

Alfredo Chicken

5 or 6 boneless, skinless chicken breast halves
1 (16 ounce) package frozen broccoli florets,
   thawed   .5 kg
1 sweet red bell pepper, seeded, chopped
1 (16 ounce) jar alfredo sauce   .5 kg

- Preheat oven to 325° (162° C).

- Brown and cook chicken breasts in large skillet with a little oil until juices run clear.

- Transfer to greased 9 x 13-inch (23 x 33 cm) baking dish.

- Microwave broccoli according to package directions and drain. (If broccoli stems are extra long, trim and discard.)

- Spoon broccoli and bell pepper over chicken.

- In small saucepan, heat alfredo sauce with ¼ cup (60 ml) water.

- Pour over chicken and vegetables. Cover and cook 15 to 20 minutes.

TIP: This chicken-broccoli dish can be "dressed up" a bit by sprinkling a little shredded parmesan cheese over the top after casserole comes out of the oven.

*Savory Chicken Fettuccine

2 pounds boneless, skinless chicken thighs, cubed	1 kg
½ teaspoon garlic powder	2 ml
1 sweet red bell pepper, chopped	
2 ribs celery, chopped	
1 (10 ounce) can cream of celery soup	280 g
1 (10 ounce) can cream of chicken soup	280 g
1 (8 ounce) package cubed processed cheese	227 g
1 (4 ounce) jar diced pimentos	114 g
1 (16 ounce) package spinach fettuccine	.5 kg

- Place chicken in slow cooker. Sprinkle with garlic powder, ½ teaspoon (2 ml) pepper, bell pepper and celery. Top with undiluted soups.

- Cover and cook on HIGH for 4 to 6 hours or until chicken juices are clear.

- Stir in cheese and pimentos. Cover and cook until cheese melts.

- Cook fettuccine according to package directions and drain.

- Place fettuccine in serving bowl and spoon chicken over fettuccine. Serve hot.

*Indicates slow cooker recipes.

*Imperial Chicken

1 (6 ounce) box long grain and wild rice	168 g
6 boneless, skinless chicken breast halves	
1 (16 ounce) jar roasted garlic-parmesan	
cheese creation	.5 kg
1 (16 ounce) box frozen French-style green	
beans, thawed	.5 kg
½ cup slivered almonds, toasted	120 ml

- Spray oblong slow cooker with vegetable cooking spray and pour in 2½ cups (600 ml) water, rice and seasoning packet and stir well.

- Add cheese and mix well. Place chicken breasts in slow cooker and cover with green beans.

- Cover and cook on LOW for 3 to 5 hours. When ready to serve, sprinkle with slivered almonds.

Chicken-Parmesan Spaghetti

1 (14 ounce) package frozen, cooked, breaded chicken	
cutlets, thawed	396 g
1 (28 ounce) jar spaghetti sauce	794 g
2 (5 ounce) packages grated parmesan cheese,	
divided	2 (143 g)
1 (8 ounce) package thin spaghetti, cooked	227 g

- Preheat oven to 400° (204° C). Place cutlets in buttered 9 x 13-inch (23 x 33 cm) baking dish and top each with about ¼ cup (60 ml) spaghetti sauce and 1 heaping tablespoon (15 ml) parmesan. Bake 15 minutes.

- Place cooked spaghetti on serving platter and top with cutlets. Sprinkle remaining cheese over cutlets. Heat remaining spaghetti sauce and serve with chicken and spaghetti.

Hawaiian Chicken

2 small, whole chickens, quartered
Flour
Oil
1 (20 ounce) can sliced pineapple with juice   567 g
2 bell peppers, cut in strips

- Wash and pat chicken dry with paper towels. Sprinkle a little salt, pepper and flour on chicken.

- Brown chicken in oil and place in shallow pan.

- Drain pineapple into 2-cup (480 ml) measure. Add water (or orange juice if you have it) to make 1½ cups (360 ml) liquid. Reserve juice for sauce.

Sauce:

1 cup sugar	240 ml
3 tablespoons cornstarch	45 ml
¾ cup vinegar	180 ml
1 tablespoon lemon juice	15 ml
1 tablespoon soy sauce	15 ml
2 teaspoons chicken bouillon	10 ml

- Combine 1½ cups (360 ml) juice, sugar, cornstarch, vinegar, lemon juice, soy sauce and chicken bouillon in medium saucepan.

- Bring to boil, stir constantly until thick and clear and pour over chicken. Bake covered at 350° (176° C) for 40 minutes.

- Place pineapple slices and bell pepper on top of chicken and bake another 10 minutes. Serve on fluffy white rice.

Almond-Crusted Chicken

1 egg	
¼ cup seasoned breadcrumbs	60 ml
1 cup sliced almonds	240 ml
4 boneless, skinless chicken breast halves	
1 (5 ounce) package grated parmesan cheese	143 g

- Preheat oven to 350° (176° C). Place egg and 1 teaspoon (5 ml) water in shallow bowl and beat. In another shallow bowl, combine breadcrumbs and almonds.

- Dip each chicken breast in egg, then in almond mixture and place in greased 9 x 13-inch (23 x 33 cm) baking pan. Bake uncovered for 20 minutes.

- Remove chicken from oven and sprinkle parmesan cheese over each breast. Cook additional 15 minutes or until almonds and cheese are golden brown.

Sauce:

2 tablespoons oil	30 ml
1 teaspoon minced garlic	5 ml
⅓ cup finely chopped onion	80 ml
1 cup white wine	240 ml
¼ cup teriyaki sauce	60 ml

- Saute garlic and onion in saucepan with a little oil. Add wine and teriyaki. Bring to boil, reduce heat and simmer about 10 minutes or until mixture reduces by half.

- When serving, divide sauce among four plates and place chicken breast on top.

*Chicken and Everything Good

2 (10 ounce) cans cream of chicken soup	2 (280 g)
⅓ cup (⅔ stick) butter, melted	80 ml
3 cups cooked, cubed chicken	710 ml
1 (16 ounce) package frozen broccoli, corn, red peppers	.5 kg
1 (10 ounce) package frozen green peas	280 g
1 (8 ounce) package cornbread stuffing mix	227 g

- Spray large slow cooker with vegetable spray. In mixing bowl, combine soup, melted butter and ⅓ cup (80 ml) water and mix well.

- Add chicken, vegetables and stuffing mix and stir well. Spoon mixture into slow cooker.

- Cover and cook on LOW for 5 to 6 hours or on HIGH for 2½ to 3 hours.

Hurry-Up Chicken Enchiladas

2½ -3 cups cooked, cubed chicken breast halves	600-710 ml
1 (10 ounce) can cream of chicken soup	280 g
1½ cups chunky salsa, divided	360 ml
8 (6-inch) flour tortillas	8 (15 cm)
1 (10 ounce) can fiesta nacho cheese soup	280 g

- Combine chicken, soup and ½ cup (120 ml) salsa in saucepan and heat. Spoon about ⅓ cup (80 ml) chicken mixture in center of each tortilla and roll tortilla.

- Place seam-side down in sprayed 9 x 13-inch (23 x 33 cm) baking dish. Mix nacho cheese, remaining salsa and ¼ cup (60 ml) water and pour over enchiladas.

- Cover with wax paper and microwave on HIGH, turning several times, for 5 minutes or until bubbly.

Catch-A-Chicken Casserole

3 cups cooked, chopped chicken or turkey	710 ml
1 (16 ounce) package frozen broccoli florets, thawed	.5 kg
1 (10 ounce) can cream of chicken soup	280 g
⅔ cup mayonnaise	160 ml
1 cup shredded cheddar cheese	240 ml
1½ cups crushed cheese crackers	360 ml

- Combine chicken, broccoli, soup mix with ¼ cup (60 ml) water, mayonnaise and cheese and mix well.

- Pour into buttered 3-quart (3 L) baking dish and spread cheese crackers over top. Bake, uncovered, at 350° (176° C) for 40 minutes.

Family Chicken Casserole

1 (7 ounce) box chicken-flavored rice and macaroni	198 g
3 cups cooked, chopped chicken or turkey	710 ml
1 (10 ounce) can cream of mushroom soup	280 g
1 (10 ounce) can cream of celery soup	280 g
1 (10 ounce) package frozen peas, thawed	280 g
1 cup shredded cheddar cheese	240 ml

- Cook rice and macaroni according to package directions.

- Combine chicken, cooked rice and macaroni, soups mixed with ½ cup (120 ml) water, peas and cheese and mix well.

- Pour into buttered 3-quart (3 L) casserole dish and bake, covered, at 350° (176° C) for 40 minutes.

Speedy Chicken Pie

*This is a "speedy" lunch that gives you extra time to
create a special "out-a-sight" dessert.*

1 (12 ounce) package shredded cheddar cheese, divided	340 g
1 (10 ounce) package frozen, chopped broccoli, thawed, drained	280 g
2 cups cooked, finely diced chicken breasts	480 ml
½ cup finely chopped onion	120 ml
½ cup finely chopped sweet red bell pepper	120 ml
1⅓ cups half-and-half cream	320 ml
3 eggs	
¾ cup biscuit mix	180 ml

- Preheat oven to 350° (176° C).

- In bowl, combine 2 cups (480 ml) cheddar cheese, broccoli, chicken, onion and bell pepper. Spread into buttered deep 10-inch (25 cm) pie plate.

- Beat cream, eggs, baking mix, 1 teaspoon (5 ml) salt and ¼ teaspoon (1 ml) pepper in mixing bowl and mix well.

- Slowly pour cream-egg mixture over broccoli-chicken mixture, but do not stir.

- Bake covered for 35 minutes or until center of pie is firm.

- Uncover and sprinkle remaining cheese over top. Return to oven for about 5 minutes or just until cheese melts.

Encore Chicken

6 boneless, skinless chicken breast halves
1 (16 ounce) jar thick, chunky hot salsa   .5 kg
1 cup packed light, brown sugar   240 ml
1 tablespoon dijon-style mustard   15 ml

- Preheat oven to 325° (162° C). In large skillet with a little oil, brown chicken breasts and place in greased 9 x 13-inch (23 x 33 cm) baking dish.

- Combine salsa, brown sugar, mustard and ½ teaspoon (2ml) salt and pour over chicken. Cover and bake 45 minutes. Serve over hot cooked brown rice.

Parmesan Chicken

1 (1 ounce) packet dry Italian salad dressing mix 28 g
½ cup parmesan cheese   120 ml
¼ cup flour   60 ml
¾ teaspoon garlic powder   4 ml
5 boneless, skinless chicken breast halves

- Preheat oven to 375° (190° C). Combine salad dressing mix, cheese, flour and garlic in shallow bowl.

- Moisten chicken with a little water and coat with cheese mixture. Place in greased 9 x 13-inch (23 x 33 cm) baking pan.

- Bake for 25 minutes or until chicken is light brown and cooks thoroughly.

Comfort Chicken Plus

1 (6 ounce) box chicken stuffing mix	168 g
1 bunch fresh broccoli florets	
1 cup chopped red bell pepper	240 ml
2 tablespoons butter	30 ml
1 (8 ounce) can whole kernel corn, drained	227 g
2½ cups finely chopped chicken or	
left-over turkey	600 ml
1 envelope (1 ounce) hollandaise sauce mix	28 g
1 (3 ounce) can french-fried onions	84 g

- Prepare chicken stuffing mix according to package directions.

- Place broccoli, celery, bell pepper, butter and ¼ cup (60 ml) water in microwave-safe bowl.

- Cover with wax paper and microwave on HIGH for 1½ minutes.

- Add broccoli-celery mixture, corn and chicken to stuffing and mix well. Spoon into buttered 8 x 12-inch (20 x 32 cm) baking dish.

- Prepare hollandaise sauce according to package directions, but use 1¼ cups (300 ml) water instead of 1 cup (240 ml) water stated.

- Pour hollandaise sauce over casserole and sprinkle top with onions.

- Bake uncovered at 325° (162° C) for 25 minutes.

Tasty Skillet Chicken

5 large boneless, skinless chicken breast halves
1 green and 1 red bell pepper, thinly sliced
2 small yellow squash, seeds removed, thinly sliced
1 (16 ounce) bottle thick, chunky salsa .5 kg
2 (9 ounce) packages ready buttery rice, cooked* 2 (255 g)

- Cut chicken breasts into thin strips. With a little oil in large skillet, saute chicken for about 5 minutes.

- Add peppers and squash and cook additional 5 minutes or until peppers are tender-crisp.

- Stir in salsa and bring to boil. Lower heat and simmer for 10 minutes. Serve over hot buttered rice.

TIP: It will take 90 seconds to cook Uncle Ben's ready buttery rice. It's a snap and great for hurry-up suppers.

To make green pepper strips or slices, hold the pepper upright on a cutting surface. Slice each side from the pepper stem and discard stem, white membrane and seeds.

Creamy Chicken Bake

1 (8 ounce) package egg noodles	227 g
1 (16 ounce) package frozen broccoli florets, thawed	.5 kg
¼ cup (½ stick) butter, melted	60 ml
1 (8 ounce) package shredded cheddar cheese	227 g
1 (10 ounce) can cream of chicken soup	280 g
1 cup half-and-half cream	240 ml
¼ teaspoon ground mustard	1 ml
3 cups cooked, cubed chicken breasts	710 ml
⅔ cup slivered almonds, toasted	160 ml

- Preheat oven to 350° (176° C).

- Cook noodles according to package directions and drain.

- Cut some stems off broccoli and discard. In large bowl, combine noodles and broccoli.

- Add butter and cheese and stir until cheese melts. Stir in chicken soup, cream, mustard, chicken and about 1 teaspoon (5 ml) each of salt and pepper.

- Spoon into buttered 2½-quart (2.5 L) baking dish.

- Bake covered for about 25 minutes and cook for 15 minutes longer.

- Remove from oven, sprinkle with slivered almonds and cool for 15 minutes longer.

Chicken Supreme
It is really delicious and "sooo" easy. It is a "meal in itself"!

1 onion, chopped	
1 cup sliced celery	240 ml
3 tablespoons butter	45 ml
4 cups diced, cooked chicken breasts	1 L
1 (6 ounce) package long grain, wild rice with seasoning	
packet, cooked	168 g
1 (10 ounce) can cream of celery soup	280 g
1 (10 ounce) can cream of chicken soup	280 g
1 (4 ounce) jar pimentos	114 g
2 (15 ounce) cans French-style green beans,	
drained	2 (425 g)
1 cup slivered almonds	240 ml
1 cup mayonnaise	240 ml
2½ cups crushed potato chips	600 ml

- Preheat oven to 350° (176° C).

- Saute onion and celery in butter. In very large saucepan, combine onion-celery mixture, diced chicken, cooked rice, both soups, pimentos, green beans, almonds, mayonnaise, ½ teaspoon (2 ml) each of salt and pepper and mix well.

- Spoon into greased 10 x 14-inch (25 x 36 cm) deep baking dish.

- Sprinkle crushed potato chips over top of casserole. Bake uncovered for 40 minutes or until potato chips are light brown.

TIP: This recipe is a great way to serve a lot of people.
It will serve at least 14 to 15. It may also be made with green peas
instead of green beans. If you want to make it in advance
and freeze or just refrigerate for the next day, just wait until you are
ready to cook the casserole before adding potato chips.

Divine Chicken Casserole

1 (16 ounce) package frozen broccoli spears,
   thawed .5 kg
1 (10 ounce) box frozen broccoli spears,
   thawed 280 g
3 cups diced, cooked chicken 710 ml
1 (10 ounce) can cream of chicken soup 280 g
2 tablespoons milk 30 ml
½ cup mayonnaise 120 ml
2 teaspoons lemon juice 10 ml
1 cup shredded cheddar cheese 240 ml
1½ cups round buttery cracker crumbs 360 ml
3 tablespoons butter, melted 45 ml

- Preheat oven to 350° (176° C).

- Cook broccoli according to package directions and drain. Cut some stems away and discard.

- Place broccoli spears in buttered 9 x 13-inch (23 x 33 cm) baking dish and sprinkle 1 teaspoon (5 ml) salt over broccoli. Cover with diced chicken.

- In saucepan, combine soup, milk, mayonnaise, lemon juice, ½ teaspoon (2 ml) pepper and cheese and heat just enough to be able to pour mixture over broccoli and chicken.

- Combine cracker crumbs and butter and sprinkle over casserole.

- Bake uncovered for 35 to 40 minutes or until hot and bubbly.

TIP: If you don't want little black specks of pepper, use white pepper instead of black pepper.

Family Night Spaghetti

6 frozen breaded, cooked chicken breast halves	
1 (8 ounce) package spaghetti, cooked	227 g
1 (18 ounce) jar spaghetti sauce	510
1 (12 ounce) package shredded mozzarella cheese, divided	340 g

- Bake chicken breasts according to package directions and keep warm. Cook spaghetti according to package directions, drain and arrange on platter.

- Place spaghetti sauce in saucepan with 1 cup (240 ml) mozzarella cheese and heat slightly, but do not boil.

- Spoon about half sauce over spaghetti and arrange chicken breast over top.

- Spoon remaining spaghetti sauce on chicken and sprinkle remaining cheese over top.

Skillet Chicken and Stuffing

1 (16 ounce) box stuffing mix for chicken with seasoning packet	.5 kg
1 (16 ounce) package frozen whole kernel corn	.5 kg
¼ cup (½ stick) butter	60 ml
4 boneless, skinless chicken breast halves, cooked	

- Combine seasoning packet, corn, 1⅔ cups (400 ml) water and butter in large skillet and bring to a boil. Reduce heat, cover and simmer for 5 minutes.

- Stir in stuffing mix just until moist. Cut chicken into thin slices and mix with stuffing-corn mixture. Cook on low heat just until mixture heats well.

Easy Chicken and Dumplings

3 cups cooked, chopped chicken	710 ml
2 (10 ounce) cans cream of chicken soup	2 (280 g)
3 teaspoons chicken bouillon granules	15 ml
1 (8 ounce) can refrigerated buttermilk biscuits	227 g

- Combine chopped chicken, both cans of soup, chicken bouillon granules and 4½ cups (1.1 L) water in large kettle or Dutch oven. Boil mixture and stir to mix well.

- Separate biscuits and cut in half, cut again making 4 pieces out of each biscuit. Drop biscuit pieces, 1 at a time, into boiling chicken mixture and stir gently.

- When all biscuits are dropped, reduce heat to low, simmer for about 15 minutes and stir occasionally.

TIP: Deli turkey will work just fine in this recipe.
It's a great time-saver!

Chicken Supper

5 boneless, skinless chicken breast halves	
5 slices onion	
5 potatoes, peeled, quartered	
1(10 ounce) can cream of celery soup	280 g

- Place chicken breasts in 9 x 13-inch (23 x 33 cm) greased baking dish.

- Top chicken with onion slices and place potatoes around chicken.

- Heat soup with ¼ cup (60 ml) water just enough to pour soup over chicken and vegetables.

- Bake covered at 325°(162° C) for 1 hour 10 minutes.

Family Chicken Bake

This is such a good, basic "meat-and-potato" dish all families love.

¼ cup (½ stick) butter	60 ml
1 sweet red bell pepper, chopped	
1 onion, chopped	
2 ribs celery, chopped	
1 (8 ounce) carton sour cream	227 g
1½ cups half-and-half cream	360 ml
1 (7 ounce) can chopped green chilies, drained	198 g
1 teaspoon chicken bouillon	5 ml
½ teaspoon celery salt	2 ml
3-4 cups cooked, cubed chicken	710-960 ml
1 (16 ounce) package shredded cheddar cheese, divided	.5 kg
1 (2 pound) package frozen hash brown potatoes, thawed	1 kg

- Melt butter in saucepan and saute bell pepper, onion and celery.

- In large bowl, combine sour cream, half-and-half, green chilies, seasonings and about ½ teaspoon (2 ml) each salt and pepper. Stir in bell pepper mixture, chicken and half of cheese. Fold in hash brown potatoes.

- Spoon into greased 9 x 13-inch (23 x 33 cm) baking dish.

- Bake, uncovered at 350° (176° C) for 45 minutes or until casserole is bubbly.

- Remove from oven and sprinkle remaining cheese over top of casserole. Return to oven for about 5 minutes.

TIP: And for a change of pace, heat some hot, thick, chunky salsa to spoon over the top of each serving.

Chicken Pot Pie

1 (15 ounce) package refrigerated piecrust	425 g
1 (19 ounce) can cream of chicken soup	538 g
2 cups diced chicken breast	480 ml
1 (10 ounce) package frozen mixed vegetables, thawed	280 g

- Preheat oven to 325° (162° C).

- Line 1 layer piecrust in 9-inch (23 cm) pie plate. Fill with chicken soup, chicken and mixed vegetables.

- Cover with second layer of piecrust, fold edges under and crimp. With knife, cut 4 slits in center of piecrust.

- Bake uncovered for 1 hour 15 minutes or until crust is golden.

TIP: When you're too busy to cook a chicken, get the rotisserie chickens from the grocery store. They are great.

Chicken-Broccoli Skillet

3 cups cubed, cooked chicken	710 ml
1 (16 ounce) package frozen broccoli florets	.5 kg
1 (8 ounce) package cubed processed cheese	227 g
⅔ cup mayonnaise	160 ml

- Combine chicken, broccoli, cheese and ¼ cup (60 ml) water in skillet. Cover and cook over medium heat until broccoli is crisp-tender and cheese melts. Stir in mayonnaise and heat through, but do not boil.

TIP: This is great served over hot cooked rice.

Cheesy Swiss Chicken

4 boneless, skinless chicken breast halves
1 (8 slices) package fully cooked bacon
4 slices Swiss cheese
⅓ cup refrigerated honey-mustard dressing   80 ml

- In large skillet with a little oil, cook chicken breasts on medium to high heat for 5 minutes.

- Remove chicken to cutting board and liberally spread each breast with honey-mustard dressing.

- Top with 2 slices bacon for each breast and cover with 1 slice Swiss cheese.

- Carefully lift each chicken breast back into skillet and place 1 tablespoon (15 ml) water in skillet. Cover and cook on low to medium heat for 10 minutes.

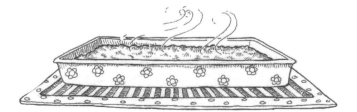

Chicken-Broccoli Bake

2 bags (3.5 ounce) white rice	100 g
1 (8 ounce) package cubed processed cheese	227 g
1 (16 ounce) package frozen broccoli florets, thawed	.5 kg
3 cups cooked, cubed chicken	710 ml
1 cup cracker crumbs or seasoned breadcrumbs	240 ml

- Preheat oven to 325° (162° C). Cook rice according to package directions. Stir in cubed cheese and ¼ cup (60 ml) water. Stir and mix until cheese melts.

- Cook broccoli according to package directions. Add broccoli and chicken to rice-cheese mixture and mix well.

- Spoon into greased 9 x 13-inch (23 x 33 cm) baking dish. Top with cracker or seasoned breadcrumbs and bake for 15 minutes.

TIP: Just use deli chicken or turkey if you don't want to cook it.

> *Good vegetable source of vitamin C are tomatoes, peppers, broccoli and cauliflower.*

Turkey Tenders with Honey-Ginger Glaze

1 pound turkey tenders	.5 kg
Lemon pepper	
Oil	

Glaze:

⅔ cup honey	160 ml
2 teaspoons grated, peeled fresh ginger	10 ml
1 tablespoon white wine Worcestershire sauce	15 ml
1 tablespoon soy sauce	15 ml
Lemon juice	

- Place a little oil in heavy skillet and cook turkey tenders about 5 minutes on each side or until brown.

- Combine all glaze ingredients, mix well and pour into skillet. Bring mixture to boil, reduce heat and simmer 15 minutes. Serve over hot cooked rice.

TIP: You might want to try the new packages of rice that you can microwave for 90 seconds and serve.

Lemon-Honey Glazed Chicken

1 (2½ -3 pound) chicken, quartered	1.2-1.3 kg
⅓ cup honey	80 ml
2 tablespoons lemon juice	30 ml
1 tablespoon dry onion soup mix	15 ml

- Preheat oven to 375° (190° C). Place chicken quarters, skin side down, on greased 9 x 13-inch (23 x 33 cm) baking pan.

- Bake uncovered for 30 minutes. Remove from oven and turn chicken quarters over.

- Combine honey, lemon juice and onion soup mix in small bowl and brush glaze over chicken. Cook, uncovered, additional 20 minutes. Brush glaze over chicken every 5 minutes.

Skillet-Roasted Chicken

1 (2½ -3 pound) chicken, quartered	1.2-1.3 kg
2 teaspoons sage	10 ml
2 teaspoons prepared minced garlic	10 ml
2 (10 ounce) cans cream of chicken soup	2 (280 g)

- Dry chicken quarters with paper towels. Sprinkle with sage and salt and pepper to taste.

- Place in large skillet with a little oil. Cook on both sides over medium to high heat for about 15 minutes.

- Combine garlic, chicken soup and ½ cup (120 ml) water in saucepan. Heat just enough to blend ingredients. Pour over chicken, cover and cook on low heat for 5 minutes or until chicken heats thoroughly. Serve over hot buttered rice.

Honey-Roasted Chicken

3 tablespoons soy sauce	45 ml
3 tablespoons honey	45 ml
2½ cups crushed wheat cereal	600 ml
½ cup very finely minced walnuts	120 ml
5 to 6 boneless, skinless chicken breast halves	

- Preheat oven to 400° (204° C). Combine soy sauce and honey in shallow bowl and set aside. In another shallow bowl, combine crushed cereal and walnuts.

- Dip both sides of each chicken breast in soy sauce-honey mixture and dredge in cereal-walnut mixture.

- Place each piece on greased foil-lined baking sheet. Bake for 25 minutes (about 35 minutes if breasts are very large).

Italian Crumb Chicken

5 to 6 boneless, skinless chicken breast halves	
¾ cup mayonnaise	180 ml
⅓ cup grated parmesan cheese	80 ml
½ cup prepared Italian seasoned breadcrumbs	120 ml

- Preheat oven to 400° (204° C). Place all chicken breasts on foil-lined baking pan. Combine mayonnaise, 2 teaspoons (10 ml) pepper and parmesan cheese in bowl and mix well.

- Spread mixture over chicken breasts and sprinkle seasoned breadcrumbs on both sides.

- Place in oven uncovered and bake 20 to 25 minutes or until it is light brown. Breasts may be served whole or sliced diagonally.

Grilled Chicken with Raspberry-Barbecue Sauce

Chicken:
1 (2½ pound) chicken, quartered   1.2 kg

Raspberry-Barbecue Sauce:
1 (12 ounce) jar seedless raspberry preserves   340 g
½ cup bottled barbecue sauce   120 ml
2 tablespoons raspberry vinegar   30 ml
2 tablespoons dijon-style mustard   30 ml

- Season chicken quarters liberally with salt and pepper. Grill chicken, covered with grill lid, over medium-high heat for about 8 minutes on each side.

- While chicken cooks, combine all sauce ingredients. Serve with remaining sauce.

- Baste with Raspberry-Barbecue sauce during the last 2 minutes of cooking. Serve with remaining sauce.

Brown Rice Chicken

2 (5 ounce) cans premium chunk chicken breasts 2 (143 g)
2 (8.8 ounce) packages whole-grain
   brown ready rice   2 (255 g)
⅔ cups sun-dried tomatoes   160 ml
2 ripe avocados, peeled, diced
¾ cup dijon-style mustard vinaigrette dressing   180 ml

- Pour broth from chicken into small bowl and save. Separate chicken into chunks. Prepare rice according to package directions.

- Combine chicken, rice, tomatoes and avocado. Combine vinaigrette dressing and ½ teaspoon (2 ml) salt.

- Gently stir into chicken-rice mixture and refrigerate 2 hours before serving.

TIP: This rice goes in the microwave and is ready in 90 seconds. Not bad for the rush hour!

Sweet-Spicy Chicken Thighs

10 to 12 chicken thighs
3 tablespoons chili powder   45 ml
3 tablespoon honey   45 ml
2 tablespoon lemon juice   30 ml

- Preheat oven to 425° (220° C). Line 10 x 15-inch (25 x 38 cm) shallow baking pan with heavy foil and set metal rack in pan.

- Combine chili powder, honey, lemon juice and lots salt and pepper.

- Brush mixture over chicken thighs and place on rack in prepared pan. Turn thighs to coat completely.

- Bake, turning over once, for about 35 minutes.

Favorite Oven-Fried Chicken

Marinade:

2 cups buttermilk	480 ml
2 tablespoons dijon-style mustard	30 ml
2 teaspoons garlic powder	10 ml
1 teaspoon cayenne pepper	5 ml

Chicken:

6 to 8 boneless, skinless chicken breast halves	
2½ cups crushed corn flakes	600 ml
¾ cup breadcrumbs	180 ml
2 tablespoons olive oil	30 ml

- Combine marinade mixture in large bowl and mix well. Place chicken pieces in bowl and turn to coat well. Place in refrigerator and marinate 2 hours or overnight.

- Preheat oven to 400° (204° C). Line large baking pan with foil and spray with cooking oil.

- In large shallow bowl, combine crushed flakes and breadcrumbs. Drizzle oil over crumbs and toss until they coat well.

- Take 1 piece chicken at a time, remove from marinade and dredge in crumb mixture. Press crumbs onto all sides of chicken and place in prepared baking pan. Do not let sides touch. Bake 35 to 40 minutes.

TIP: The easiest way to crush corn flakes is in a sealed plastic bag and the palm of your hand. You don't even have to get out the rolling pin if you don't want to or don't have one. Who needs a rolling pin anyway?

Chicken and Noodles

1 (3 ounce) package chicken-flavored,
   instant ramen noodles   84 g
1 (16 ounce) package frozen broccoli,
   cauliflower and carrots   .5 kg
⅔ cup sweet-and-sour sauce   160 ml
3 boneless, skinless chicken breast halves, cooked

- Cook noodles and vegetables in saucepan with 2 cups (480 ml) boiling water for 3 minutes, stir occasionally and drain.

- Combine noodle-vegetable mixture with seasoning packet, sweet-and-sour sauce and a little salt and pepper. Cut chicken in strips, add chicken to noodle mixture and heat thoroughly.

*TIP: You may want to add 1 tablespoon (15 ml)
soy sauce if you have it on hand.*

Glazed Chicken and Rice

4 boneless, skinless chicken breast halves, cubed
1 (20 ounce) can pineapple chunks with juice   567 g
½ cup honey mustard grill-and-glaze sauce   120 ml
1 red bell pepper, chopped
Rice, cooked

- In skillet with a little oil, brown chicken cook on low heat for 15 minutes and turn once. Add pineapple, honey mustard and bell pepper and bring to boil.

- Reduce heat to low and simmer for 10 to 15 minutes or until sauce thickens slightly. Serve over hot cooked rice.

Super Chicken Spaghetti

This recipe is a little different twist on the long-time favorite chicken spaghetti. This is a wonderful casserole to serve to family or for company. It has great flavor with chicken, pasta and colorful vegetables all in one dish. It's a winner, I promise!

1 bunch fresh green onions with tops, chopped	
1 cup chopped celery	240 ml
1 red and 1 yellow bell pepper, chopped	
¼ cup (½ stick) butter	60 ml
1 tablespoon dried cilantro leaves	15 ml
1 teaspoon Italian seasoning	5 ml
1 (7 ounce) package thin spaghetti, cooked, drained	198 g
4 cups chopped, cooked chicken or turkey	1 L
1 (8 ounce) carton sour cream	227 g
1 (16 ounce) jar creamy alfredo sauce	.5 kg
1 (10 ounce) box frozen green peas, thawed	280 g
1 (8 ounce) package shredded mozzarella cheese, divided	227 g

- Saute onions, celery and bell peppers in butter in large skillet.

- In large bowl combine onion-pepper mixture, cilantro, Italian seasonings, spaghetti, chicken, sour cream and alfredo sauce and mix well.

- Sprinkle a little salt and pepper in mixture. Fold in peas and half mozzarella cheese.

- Spoon into greased 10 x 14-inch (25 x 36 cm) deep casserole dish and bake covered at 350° (176° C) for 45 minutes.

- Remove from oven and sprinkle remaining cheese over casserole. Return to oven for about 5 minutes.

*Cornish Hens with Ginger-Orange Glaze

Glaze:
1 cup fresh orange juice	240 ml
2 tablespoons peeled, minced fresh ginger	30 ml
1 tablespoon soy sauce	15 ml
3 tablespoons honey	45 ml

Cornish Hens:
2 (1½ pounds) Cornish hens, halved	2 (680 g)
½ teaspoon ground ginger	

- Preheat oven to 450° (230° C).

- Combine orange juice, minced ginger, soy sauce and honey in saucepan and cook on high heat, stirring constantly, for 3 minutes or until thick and glossy.

- Place hens in greased baking pan and sprinkle ground ginger and ½ teaspoon (2 ml) each of salt and pepper over birds.

- Spoon glaze mixture over hens and bake 25 minutes. Brush glaze over hens several times during cooking.

*Indicates slow cooker recipes.

*Turkey Cassoulet

This is a great recipe for leftover turkey.

2 cups cooked turkey, cubed	480 ml
8 ounces smoked turkey sausage	227 g
3 carrots, sliced	
1 onion, halved, sliced	
1 (15 ounce) can navy bean	425 g
1 (15 ounce) white lima beans	425 g
1 (8 ounce) can tomato sauce	227 g
1 teaspoon dried thyme	5 ml
¼ teaspoon ground allspice	1 ml

- Cut turkey sausage in ½-inch (1.2 cm) pieces.

- Combine all ingredients in slow cooker sprayed with vegetable cooking spray.

- Cover and cook on LOW for 4 to 5 hours.

Turkey-Rice Olé

This may be served as a 1-dish meal or as a sandwich wrap in flour tortillas.

1 pound ground turkey	.5 kg
1 (5.5 ounce) package Mexican rice mix	155 g
1 (15 ounce) can black beans, rinsed, drained	425 g
1 cup thick, chunky salsa	240 ml

- Brown turkey in large skillet and break up large pieces with fork. Add rice mix and 2 cups (480 ml) water.

- Bring to boiling, reduce heat and simmer about 8 minutes or until rice is tender.

- Stir in beans and salsa and cook just until mixture heats through.

Turkey and Ham Tetrazzini

This is another old-fashioned dish modified for today's
"hurry-up meal", but it keeps the same great taste.

½ cup slivered almonds, toasted	120 ml
1 (10 ounce) can cream of mushroom soup	280 g
1 (10 ounce) can cream of chicken soup	280 g
¾ cup milk	180 ml
2 tablespoons dry white wine	30 ml
1 (7 ounce) box thin spaghetti, cooked, drained	198 g
2½ cups diced, cook left-over turkey	600 ml
2 cups fully cooked, left-over diced ham	480 ml
½ cup chopped green bell pepper	120 ml
½ cup chopped sweet red bell pepper	120 ml
½ cup halved pitted ripe olives	120 ml
1 (8 ounce) package shredded cheddar cheese	227 g

- Preheat oven to 350° (176° C). Mix almonds, both soups, milk and wine in large bowl.

- Stir in spaghetti, turkey, ham, chopped peppers and pitted olives. Spoon into buttered 9 x 13-inch (23 x 33 cm) baking dish.

- Bake covered for 35 minutes or until casserole is hot and bubbly.

- Remove cover and sprinkle top of casserole with cheese. Return to oven for 5 minutes.

Turkey-Asparagus Alfredo

1 bunch fresh asparagus
1 sweet red bell pepper, thinly sliced
1 (16 ounce) carton alfredo sauce .5 kg
½ pound deli smoked turkey 227 g

- Bring ½ cup (120 ml) water to boil. Cut off woody ends of asparagus and cut into thirds.

- Add asparagus and bell peppers to skillet, cook on medium to high heat for 4 minutes or until tender-crisp and drain.

- Slice turkey in thin strips. With skillet still on medium to high heat, stir in alfredo sauce and turkey strips.

- Bring to boil, reduce heat and simmer until mixture heats thoroughly.

Caribbean Turkey

Turkey tenderloins are wonderful. You will be glad you cooked them!

2 tablespoons jerk seasoning	30 ml
1½ to 2 pounds turkey tenderloins	.7-1 kg
1 tablespoons fresh chopped rosemary	15 ml
1½ cups raspberry-chipotle sauce	360 ml

- Rub jerk seasoning evenly over tenderloins, sprinkle with rosemary and press into tenderloins. Cover and refrigerate for 1 to 2 hours.

- Grill tenderloins with lid closed, over medium-high heat for 5-10 minutes on each side. Baste with half the raspberry-chipotle sauce.

- Let tenderloin stand 10 minutes before slicing and serve with remaining raspberry-chipotle sauce.

Turkey Pasta

3 ounces twisted noodles	84 g
1 (1 ounce) package ranch salad dressing mix	28 g
¾ cup mayonnaise	180 ml
1 cup milk	240 ml
3 cups cooked, diced turkey	710 ml
1 (10 ounce) package frozen peas	280 g
1 (4 ounce) can chopped green chilies	114 g
¾ cup cracker crumbs	180 ml

- Cook noodles according to package directions. Combine salad dressing mix, mayonnaise and milk in large mixing bowl. Add turkey, peas and green chilies and mix well.

- Drain noodles, add to turkey mixture and toss. Pour into greased 3-quart (3 L) baking dish. Cook covered at 350° (176° C) for 25 minutes. Uncover and sprinkle cracker crumbs over top of casserole. Return to oven for another 10 or 15 minutes.

Easy
Powerful
Pork

Sweet Peach Pork Tenderloin

3 tablespoons dijon-style mustard	45 ml
1 tablespoon soy sauce	15 ml
1 (12 ounce) jar peach preserves	340 g
2 (1 pound) pork tenderloins	2 (.5 kg)

- Preheat oven to 325° (162° C).

- Combine mustard, soy sauce and peach preserves in saucepan. Heat and stir just until mixture blends.

- Place tenderloins in greased baking pan and spoon peach mixture over top.

- Sprinkle a little salt and black pepper over tenderloin.

- Cover pan with foil, bake for 1 hour and remove from oven.

- Remove foil covering and return to oven for 25 minutes. Let sit at room temperature for about 15 minutes before slicing.

When selecting pork, look for meat that is pale pink with a small amount of marbling and white fat (not yellow). The darker pink the flesh appears, the older the animal.

Pork Tenderloin
With Cranberry Sauce

2 (1 pound) pork tenderloins	2 (.5 kg)
½ cup chopped fresh cilantro	120 ml
½ teaspoon ground cumin	2 ml
2 teaspoons minced garlic	10 ml

- Preheat oven to 375° (190° C).

- Season tenderloin with a little salt and pepper, cilantro, cumin and garlic.

- Place in foil-lined baking pan and bake 15 minutes.

- Reduce heat to 325° (162° C) and bake another 35 minutes. Slice to serve.

Cranberry Sauce:

1 (16 ounce) can whole cranberries	.5 kg
1 cup orange marmalade	240 ml
1 (8 ounce) can crushed pineapple, drained	227 g
¾ cup chopped pecans	180 ml

- For cranberry sauce, combine cranberries, marmalade, pineapple and pecans and serve with tenderloin.

- Sauce may be served room temperature or warmed.

Grilled Pork Tenderloin with Rice

2 (1 pound) pork tenderloins	2 (.5 kg)
1 tablespoon oil	15 ml
2 tablespoons jerk seasoning	30 ml

- Rub tenderloins with oil and sprinkle with jerk seasoning.

- Grill over medium to high heat about 25 minutes, brown on both sides and cook until meat thermometer inserted in center registers 160° (71° C).

Rice and Beans:

1 (6 ounce) package chicken-flavored rice	168 g
1 (15 ounce) can black beans, rinsed	425 g
½ cup roasted red bell pepper, sliced	120 ml
2 tablespoons chopped cilantro	30 ml

- Cook rice according to package directions. Add beans, bell pepper, cilantro and salt and pepper to taste. Spoon on serving platter.

- Slice tenderloin and arrange on top of rice-bean mixture.

Fiesta-Pork Casserole

This zesty casserole is so easy to put together and it really gets your attention! It is an especially nice change of pace from the usual Mexican dish with ground beef.

2 pounds boneless pork tenderloin	1 kg
1 onion, chopped	
1 green bell pepper, chopped	
3 tablespoons oil	45 ml
1 (15 ounce) can black beans, rinsed, drained	425 g
1 (10 ounce) can fiesta nacho cheese	280 g
1 (15 ounce) can stewed tomatoes	425 g
1 (4 ounce) can chopped green chilies	114 g
1 cup instant brown rice, cooked	240 ml
¾ cup salsa	180 ml
2 teaspoons ground cumin	10 ml
½ teaspoon garlic powder	2 ml
¾ cup shredded Mexican 3-cheese blend	180 ml

- Preheat oven to 350° (176° C).

- Cut pork into 1-inch (2.5 cm) cubes. In very large skillet, brown and cook pork, onion and bell pepper in oil until pork is no longer pink. Drain.

- Add beans, fiesta nacho cheese soup, stewed tomatoes, green chilies, rice, salsa, cumin, ½ teaspoon (2 ml) salt and garlic powder to skillet.

- Cook on medium heat, stirring occasionally, until mixture bubbles.

- Spoon into buttered 4-quart (4 L) baking dish. Bake uncovered for 30 minutes or until it bubbles around edges.

- Remove from oven and sprinkle with cheese. Let stand a few minutes before serving.

One-Dish Pork and Peas

So many of our casseroles are chicken, but pork is so good and always tender. This blend of ingredients makes a delicious dish.

1½ pounds pork tenderloin	.7 kg
2 tablespoons oil	30 ml
1 cup sliced celery	240 ml
1 onion, chopped	
1 sweet red bell pepper, chopped	
1 (8 ounce) package small egg noodles, cooked, drained	227 g
1 (10 ounce) can cream of chicken soup	280 g
½ cup half-and-half cream	120 ml
1 (10 ounce) package frozen green peas, thawed	280 g
1 cup seasoned dry breadcrumbs	240 ml
⅓ cup chopped walnuts	80 ml

- Preheat oven to 350° (176° C).

- Cut pork into ½-inch (1.2 cm) cubes. In large skillet, brown cubed pork in oil. Reduce heat and cook for about 20 minutes. Remove pork to separate dish.

- In remaining oil saute celery, onion and bell pepper.

- Add pork, noodles, soup, cream, peas, about 1 teaspoon (5 ml) salt and ½ teaspoon (2 ml) pepper.

- Spoon into buttered 3-quart (3 L) baking dish. Sprinkle with breadcrumbs and walnuts.

- Bake uncovered for about 25 minutes or until it bubbles.

Pork and Noodles Supreme

2 tablespoons oil	30 ml
2 pounds pork tenderloin, cut into 1-inch cubes	1 kg
2 ribs celery, chopped	
1 red and 1 green bell pepper, chopped	
1 onion, chopped	
1 (12 ounce) package medium egg noodles, cooked, drained	340 g
1 (10 ounce) can cream of celery soup	280 g
1 (10 ounce) can cream of chicken soup	280 g
1 (15 ounce) can creamed corn	425 g
¾ cup half-and-half cream	180 ml
1½ cups crushed corn flakes	360 ml
3 tablespoons butter, melted	45 ml

- Preheat oven to 350° (176° C). In skillet, heat oil, brown and cook pork about 15 minutes. Spoon pork into large bowl.

- With remaining oil in skillet, saute celery, bell pepper and onion. Spoon into bowl with pork.

- Add noodles, both soups, creamed corn, half-and-half, and ½ teaspoon (2 ml) each of salt and pepper to pork in bowl.

- Mix well and pure into buttered 9 x 13-inch (23 x 33 cm) baking dish.

- Combine crushed corn flakes and butter and sprinkle over casserole. Bake covered for about 30 minutes.

TIP: It may be hard to find a 1½-pound pork roast, so just buy a 1½-pound pork tenderloin. It is a little more expensive, but well worth it because you are not buying bones and the tenderloin will be tender and delicious.

Oodles of Noodles

1½-2 pounds pork tenderloin,	.7-1 kg
3 tablespoons oil	45 ml
2 cups chopped celery	480 ml
1 red and 1 green bell pepper, chopped	
1 onion, chopped	
1 (4 ounce) can sliced mushrooms	114 g
1 (10 ounce) can tomatoes and green chilies	280 g
1 (10 ounce) can cream of mushroom soup	
with garlic	280 g
1 (10 ounce) can cream of celery soup	280 g
¼ cup soy sauce	60 ml
1 (7 ounce) package elbow macaroni, cooked,	
drained	198 g
2 cups chow mein noodles	480 ml

- Preheat oven to 350° (176° C).

- Cut pork into 1-inch (2.5 cm) cubes. In skillet, brown pork in oil and cook on low heat for about 15 minutes. Remove pork with slotted spoon to side dish.

- Saute celery, bell peppers and onion in same skillet in remaining oil.

- In large bowl, combine pork, celery-onion mixture, mushrooms, tomatoes and green chilies, soups, soy sauce and macaroni. Spoon casserole into large, buttered 9 x 13-inch (23 x 33 cm) baking dish or 2 smaller baking dishes.

- Top with chow mein noodles. Bake uncovered for 50 minutes.

TIP: If you make 2 smaller casseroles, you may freeze one. Wait to sprinkle the chow mein noodles over casserole until just before you place it in the oven to cook.

Sweet Potato Ham

1 (16 ounce/½-inch) thick, fully cooked ham slice	.5 kg/1.2 cm
1 (18 ounce) can sweet potatoes, drained	510 g
½ cup packed brown sugar	120 ml
⅓ cup chopped pecans	80 ml

- Cut outer edge of ham fat at 1-inch (2.5 cm) intervals to prevent curling, but do not cut into ham.

- Place on 10-inch (25 cm) microwave-safe pie plate and broil with top 5 inches from heat for 5 minutes.

- Mash each piece of sweet potatoes in bowl with fork just once (not totally mashed) and add brown sugar, a little salt and chopped pecans and mix well.

- Spoon mixture over ham slice and cook at 350° (176° C) for about 15 minutes. Serve right from microwave-safe pie plate.

Pork Chop Casserole

6 (¾ inch) boneless pork chops	6 (1.8 cm)
2 tablespoons oil	30 ml
1 green and 1 yellow bell pepper, chopped	
1 (15 ounce) can tomato sauce	425 g
1 (15 ounce) can Italian stewed tomatoes	425 g
1 teaspoon minced garlic	5 ml
1½ cups uncooked long grain rice	360 ml

- Preheat oven to 350° (176° C).

- Sprinkle pork chops with about ½ teaspoon (2 ml) each of salt and pepper.

- In skillet, brown pork chops in oil. Remove chops from skillet and set aside.

- Cut top off green pepper, remove seeds, cut 6 rings from green bell pepper and set aside.

- Combine chopped yellow pepper, tomato sauce, Italian stewed tomatoes, 1 cup (240 ml) water, onion, garlic and ½ teaspoon (2 ml) salt in separate bowl and stir well.

- Spread rice in greased 9 x 13-inch (23 x 33 cm) baking dish and slowly pour tomato mixture over rice.

- Arrange pork chops over rice and place pepper ring over each chop.

- Cover and bake for 1 hour or until chops and rice are tender.

Pork Chop Supper

1 (18 ounce) package smoked pork chops	510 g
1 (12 ounce) jar pork gravy	340 g
¼ cup milk	60 ml
1 (12 ounce) package very small new potatoes	340 g

- Brown pork chops in large skillet with a little oil. Pour gravy and milk or water into skillet and stir mixture around chops until they mix well.

- Add new potatoes around chops and gravy. Place lid on skillet and simmer on low to medium heat for about 15 minutes or until potatoes are tender.

TIP: The (18 ounce/510 g) package pork chops will give you about 5-6 chops if they are the average size.

Easy Pork Stew

This is great with cornbread!

1 (1 pound) pork tenderloin, cubed	.5 kg
2 (12 ounce) jars pork gravy	2 (340 g)
¼ cup chili sauce	60 ml
1 (16 ounce) package frozen stew vegetables, thawed	.5 kg

- Cook pork pieces in greased soup pot on medium-high heat for 10 minutes, stirring frequently.

- Stir in gravy, chili sauce and stew vegetables and bring to boil. Reduce heat and simmer for 12 minutes or until vegetables are tender.

Parmesan-Covered Pork Chops

½ cup grated parmesan cheese	120 ml
⅔ cup Italian seasoned dried breadcrumbs	160 ml
1 egg	
4 or 5 thin-cut pork chops	

- Combine cheese and dried breadcrumbs in shallow bowl. Beat egg with 1 teaspoon (5 ml) water on shallow plate.

- Dip each pork chop in beaten egg then into breadcrumb mixture.

- Cook over medium to high heat in skillet with a little oil for about 5 minutes on each side or until golden brown.

Marinated Garlic-Herb Tenderloin

2 (1 pound) pork tenderloins	2 (.5 kg)
1 (12 ounce) bottle roasted garlic and herb marinade, divided	340 g
1 (8 ounce) package medium egg noodles	227 g
¼ cup (½ stick) butter	60 ml

- Butterfly pork lengthwise, being careful not to cut all the way through. Press open to flatten and place in large plastic bag with seal. Pour ¾ cup (180 ml) marinade into bag and close top securely. Marinate for 25 minutes and turn several times.

- Grill 4 to 5 inches from hot coals for 8 minutes.

- Turn pork over and brush with additional marinade and cook another 8 minutes.

Pork Chops
With Black Bean Salsa

2 teaspoons chili powder   10 ml
2 tablespoons vegetable oil   30 ml
6 boneless thin-cut pork chops

- Combine chili powder and ½ teaspoon (2 ml) salt. Rub oil over pork chops and rub chili powder mixture over chops.

- Place in skillet over medium heat and cook pork chops about 5 minutes on both sides.

Black Bean Salsa:

1 (15 ounce) can black beans, rinsed, drained   425 g
1 (24 ounce) refrigerated citrus fruit, drained 680 g
1 ripe avocado, sliced
⅔ cup Italian salad dressing   160 ml

- For salsa, combine beans, fruit and avocado and toss with salad dressing. Serve with pork chops.

If you want succulent chops, choose those that are about 1-inch thick. Thinner chops will tend to dry out no matter how careful you are about cooking them.

Onion-Smothered Pork Chops

1 tablespoon oil	15 ml
6 (½-inch thick) pork chops	6 (1.2 cm)
1 onion, chopped	
2 tablespoons butter	30 ml
1 (10 ounce) can cream of onion soup	280 g

- Brown pork chops in oil in skillet, simmer about 10 minutes and place pork chops in greased shallow baking pan.

- Add butter in same skillet and saute chopped onion. (Pan juices are brown from pork chops so onions will be brown.)

- Add onion soup and ½ cup (120 ml) water and stir well. (Sauce will have a pretty, light brown color.) Pour onion soup mixture over pork chops. Cover, bake at 325° (162° C) for 40 minutes and serve over brown rice.

Pork-Potato Chop

6 boneless or loin pork chops	
1 (14 ounce) can chicken broth	396 g
2 (1 ounce) packages dry onion gravy mix	2 (28 g)
4 red potatoes, sliced	

- Seasoned chops with a little salt and pepper and brown in large skillet with a little oil. Combine chicken broth and gravy mix. Add potatoes to skillet with pork chops and cover with gravy mixture.

- Heat to boil, cover and simmer 45 minutes or until pork chops and potatoes are fork-tender.

*Pork Chops and Gravy

6 (½-inch) thick pork chops	6 (1.2 cm)
8-10 new potatoes with peel, quartered	
1 (16 ounce) package baby carrots	1 (.5 g)
2 (10 ounce) cans cream of mushroom soup with roasted garlic	2 (280 g)

- Sprinkle a little salt and pepper on pork chops.

- In skillet, brown pork chops and place in 5 to 6-quart (6 L) slow cooker. Place potatoes and carrots around pork chops.

- In saucepan, heat mushroom soup with ½ cup (120 ml) water and pour over chops and vegetables.

- Cover and cook in slow cooker on LOW for 6 to 7 hours.

*Indicates slow cooker recipes.

Pork Chops, Potatoes and Green Beans

6 - 8 boneless or loin pork chops
2 (1 ounce) packets gravy mix or   2 (28 g)
2 (12 ounce) jars prepared gravy   2 (340 g)
2 (15 ounce) cans white potatoes, drained   2 (425 g)
2 (15 ounce) cans cut green beans, drained   2 (425 g)

- Season pork chops with salt and pepper if desired

- Brown pork chops over medium heat in large, prepared, non-stick Dutch oven.

- Mix gravy with water according to package directions or pour prepared gravy over pork chops.

- Cover and simmer for 30 minutes.

- Add potatoes and green beans and simmer about 10 minutes or until pork chops are tender and green beans and potatoes are hot.

Ham-it Up Supper

This is really simple to put together and the kids will be ready to eat their vegetables when ham and cheese are in the picture.

1 (6 ounce) package instant long grain, wild rice	168 g
1 (10 ounce) package frozen broccoli spears, thawed	280 g
1 (8 ounce) can whole kernel corn, drained	227 g
3 cups cubed, fully cooked ham	710 ml
1 (10 ounce) can cream of mushroom soup	280 g
1 cup mayonnaise	240 ml
1 teaspoon prepared mustard	5 ml
1 cup shredded cheddar cheese	240 ml
1 (3 ounce) can fried onion rings	84 g

- Prepare rice according to package directions.

- Preheat oven to 350° (176° C). Spoon into buttered 3-quart (3 L) baking dish. Top with broccoli, corn and ham.

- Combine soup, mayonnaise, mustard, shredded cheese and ½ teaspoon (2 ml) each of salt and pepper in saucepan and mix well. Spread over top of rice-ham mixture.

- Cover and bake for about 30 minutes. Remove from oven and sprinkle onion rings over top.

- Return to oven, uncovered, and bake another 15 minutes or until casserole bubbles around edges and onion rings are light brown.

TIP: What a great way to use leftover ham, all the little slivers and chunks left from those nice big slices.

Fruit-Covered Ham Slice

2 (15 ounce) cans fruit cocktail with juice	2 (425 g)
½ cup packed brown sugar	120 ml
2 tablespoons cornstarch	30 ml
1 (½-inch) thick center-cut ham slice	1 (1.2 cm)

- Combine fruit cocktail, brown sugar and cornstarch and mix well. Cook on medium heat, stirring frequently, until sauce thickens.

- Place ham slice in large non-stick skillet on medium heat. Cook about 5 minutes or just until ham thoroughly heats.

- Place on serving platter and spoon fruit sauce over ham.

Peach-Glazed Ham

1 (5 pound) boneless ham	2.2 kg
1 (12 ounce) jar peach preserves	340 g
3 tablespoons dijon-style mustard	45 ml
¼ cup packed brown sugar	60 ml

- Cook ham according to label directions. Combine preserves, mustard and brown sugar and mix well.

- About 30 minutes before cooking time ends, remove ham from oven and drain any liquid.

- Brush ham with preserve-sugar mixture and return to oven for 30 minutes.

- Heat remaining preserve-sugar mixture in saucepan. Serve ham with heated preserve-sugar mixture.

Noodles and Ham With Veggies

1 (8 ounce) package medium egg noodles	227 g
1 (10 ounce) can cream of celery soup	280 g
1 (10 ounce) can cream of broccoli soup	280 g
1 teaspoon chicken bouillon	5 ml
1½ cups half-and-half cream	360 ml
1 (8 ounce) can whole kernel corn, drained	227 g
1 (16 ounce) package frozen broccoli, cauliflower and carrots, thawed	.5 kg
3 cups cooked cubed ham	710 ml
1 (8 ounce) package shredded cheddar-jack cheese, divided	227 g

- Cook noodles according to package directions and drain. Preheat oven to 350° (176° C).

- In large bowl, combine soups, chicken bouillon, cream, corn, broccoli-carrot mixture, ham, ½ teaspoon (2 ml) salt and 1 teaspoon (5 ml) pepper and mix well.

- Fold in egg noodles and half of cheese. Spoon into greased 9 x 13-inch (23 x 33 cm) baking dish. Cover and bake for 45 minutes.

- Uncover and sprinkle remaining cheese over top of casserole.

- Return to oven and bake another 10 minutes or until cheese bubbles.

Ham and Potatoes Olé!

1 (24 ounce) package frozen hash browns with onion and peppers, thawed	680 g
3 cups cubed, cooked ham	710 ml
1 (10 ounce) can cream of chicken soup	280 g
1 (10 ounce) can fiesta nacho cheese soup	280 g
1 cup hot salsa	240 ml
1 (8 ounce) package shredded cheddar-jack cheese	227 g

- Preheat oven to 350° (176° C). In large bowl, combine potatoes, ham, both soups and salsa and mix well. Spoon into buttered 9 x 13-inch (23 x 33 cm) baking dish.

- Cover and cook for 40 minutes. Remove from oven, sprinkle cheese over casserole and bake uncovered another 5 minutes.

Supper-in-a-Dish

2 (9 ounce) packages rice in-a-bag	2 (255 g)
1½ cups cubed, cooked ham	360 ml
1½ cups shredded cheddar cheese	360 ml
1 (8 ounce) can green peas	227 g

- Prepare rice according to package directions. In large bowl, combine rice, ham, cheese and peas.

- Pour into 3-quart (3 L) baking dish and bake at 350° (176° C) for 15 to 20 minutes.

Tortellini-Ham Supper

This is another great recipe for leftover ham.

2 (9 ounce) packages fresh tortellini	2 (255 g)
1 (10 ounce) package frozen green peas, thawed	280 g
1 (16 ounce) jar alfredo sauce	.5 kg
2-3 cups cubed ham	480-710 ml

- Cook tortellini according to package directions. Add green peas about 5 minutes before tortellini are done and drain.

- In saucepan, combine alfredo sauce and ham and heat until thoroughly hot. Toss with tortellini and peas. Serve immediately.

Ham and Sweet Potatoes

3 tablespoons dijon-style mustard, divided	45 ml
1 (3 to 4 pounds) boneless smoke ham	1.3-1.5 kg
½ cup honey or packed brown sugar	120 ml
1 (29 ounce) can sweet potatoes, drained	804 g

- Preheat oven to 325° (162° C).

- Spread mustard on ham. Place ham in prepared, shallow baking pan and bake for 20 minutes.

- Combine remaining mustard with brown sugar or honey and spread over ham. Add sweet potatoes, baste with sauce and bake for 20 minutes.

Broiled Ham
with Sweet Potatoes

1 (½-inch) thick fully cooked, center-cut ham slice	1.2 cm
1 (15 ounce) can sweet potatoes, drained	425 g
½ cup packed brown sugar	120 ml
2 tablespoons melted butter	30 ml
1 teaspoon ground cinnamon	5 ml

- Cut edges of ham fat at 1-inch (2.5 cm) intervals to prevent curling. Place ham on broiler pan and broil about 5 minutes.

- Spoon sweet potatoes into shallow dish, mash with fork and stir in brown sugar, butter and cinnamon.

- Spoon sweet potato mixture over ham and place under broiler. Broil about 5 minutes or until sweet potatoes are hot, brown and tender.

Ham and Veggies

2 (15 ounce) packages mixed vegetables	2 (425 g)
1 (10 ounce) can cream of celery soup	280 g
2 cups cubed, cooked ham	480 ml
½ teaspoon dried basil	2 ml

- Cook vegetables according to package directions. Add soup, ham and basil.

- Cook until mixture heats well and serve hot.

Bow-Tie Pasta
With Ham and Veggies

This is a great for leftover ham.

1 (8 ounce) package farfalle (bow-tie) pasta	227 g
1 (10 ounce) package frozen broccoli florets, thawed	280 g
1 (10 ounce) package frozen green peas, thawed	280 g
1 (16 ounce) jar alfredo sauce	.5 kg
1 pound cubed, cooked ham or deli ham	.5 kg

- In large saucepan, cook pasta according to package directions. Add broccoli and peas during last 3 minutes of cooking time. Drain well.

- Add alfredo sauce and ham. Cook and stir gently over very low heat to keep ingredients from sticking to pan. Pour into serving bowl.

*Uncle Ben's Ham and Rice

1 (7 ounce) box brown and wild rice, mushroom recipe	198 g
3-4 cups chopped or cubed, cooked ham	750 ml-1 L
1 (4 ounce) can sliced mushrooms, drained	114 g
1 (10 ounce) package frozen green peas	280 g
2 cups chopped celery	480 ml

- In 4 to 5-quart (5 L) slow cooker, combine rice, seasoning packet, ham, mushrooms, peas, celery plus 2⅔ cups (640 ml) water. Stir to mix well. Cover and cook in slow cooker on LOW for 2 to 4 hours.

German-Style Ribs and Kraut

3 to 4 pounds baby-back pork ribs or country-style pork ribs, trimmed	1.3-1.8 kg
3 potatoes, peeled, cubed or sliced	
1 (32 ounce) jar refrigerated sauerkraut, drained	1 kg
¼ cup pine nuts, toasted	60 ml

- Brown ribs on all sides in prepared Dutch oven. Pepper ribs to taste and add 1 cup (240 ml) water. Bring to boil, turn down heat and simmer 2 hours or until ribs are very tender.

- Add potatoes and cook on low heat for 20 minutes. Add jar of sauerkraut and continue cooking until potatoes are done.

- Sprinkle pine nuts or caraway seeds on ribs and kraut immediately before serving.

TIP: To toast pine nuts, place nuts in skillet on medium heat and stir constantly until golden brown. You may also put them on a baking sheet and cook at 300° (148° C) for 5 to 10 minutes.

Oven-Roasted Baby-Backs

⅓ cup orange juice	80 ml
⅓ cup soy sauce	80 ml
1 teaspoon ground cumin	5 ml
½ cup packed brown sugar	120 ml
2-3 pounds baby back pork ribs	1-1.3 kg

• Preheat oven to 350° (176° C). Combine orange juice, soy sauce, cumin and brown sugar in large sealable plastic bag. Shake or mash bag to blend thoroughly and to dissolve brown sugar.

• Cut ribs into individual rib, add to bag and marinate 1 to 2 hours.

• Transfer ribs and marinade to shallow baking pan and arrange in 1 layer. Ribs should not touch.

• Bake uncovered 45 minutes. Remove from oven, turn ribs with tongs and continue roasting another 30 minutes. Marinade will be thick and syrupy.

*Indicates slow cooker recipes.

Hot Pasta Frittata

½ cup chopped onion	120 ml
1 green and 1 red bell pepper, chopped	
3 tablespoons butter	45 ml
1 (7 ounce) box thin spaghetti, slightly broken,	
cooked	198 g
1½ cups shredded mozzarella cheese	360 ml
5 eggs	
½ cup milk	120 ml
⅓ cup grated parmesan cheese	80 ml
1 tablespoon basil	15 ml
1 teaspoon oregano	5 ml
2 cups diced ham	480 ml

- Preheat oven to 375° (190° C). Saute onion and bell peppers in butter in skillet over medium heat for about 5 minutes, but do not brown.

- In large bowl combine onion-pepper mixture and spaghetti and toss. Add mozzarella cheese and toss.

- In separate bowl, beat eggs, milk, parmesan cheese, basil, oregano, about ½ teaspoon salt and pepper. Add spaghetti mixture, diced ham and pour into buttered 9 x 13-inch (23 x 33 cm) baking pan or 2-quart (2L) baking dish.

- Cover with foil and bake for 10 minutes. Uncover to make sure eggs are set. If not, bake for 2 to 3 minutes longer. Cut into squares. Serves 8.

TIP: This can be prepared, chilled and baked later. Let it get to room temperature before heating.

Fettuccine Supreme

1 (8 ounce) package fettuccine	227 g
½ cup whipping cream	120 ml
½ cup (1 stick) butter, sliced	120 ml
½ teaspoon dried basil	2 ml
1 tablespoon dried parsley	15 ml
1 cup grated parmesan cheese	240 ml
1 cup diced ham	240 ml

- Cook fettuccine according to package directions and drain. Immediately place fettuccine back into saucepan.

- Add whipping cream, butter, basil, diced ham, parsley and ¼ teaspoon (1 ml) salt and toss until butter melts. Fold in parmesan cheese, pour into serving bowl and serve hot. Serves 8.

**Creamy Potatoes and Ham*

5 medium potatoes, peeled, sliced, divided	
1 teaspoon seasoned salt, divided	5 ml
1 onion, chopped, divided	
2 cups cooked, cubed ham, divided	480 ml
1 (8 ounce) package cubed processed cheese, divided	227 g
1 (10 ounce) can broccoli cheese soup	280 g
¼ cup milk	60 ml

- In slow cooker, layer half each of potatoes, seasoned salt, onion, ham and cheese and repeat layer.

- In bowl, combine soup and milk until fairly smooth and pour over potato mixture. Cover and cook on HIGH for 1 hour. Reduce heat to LOW and cook for 6 to 7 hours.

*Indicates slow cooker recipes.

Colorful Veggie Salad

4 cups fresh broccoli florets	1 L
4 cups fresh cauliflower florets	1 L
1 red onion, sliced	
1 (4 ounce) can sliced ripe olives	114 g
3 small zucchini, sliced	
2 cups chopped ham	480 ml

- In large bowl, combine broccoli, cauliflower, onion, olives, zucchini, chopped ham and toss.

Dressing:

1 (.6 ounces) envelope zesty Italian dry dressing mix	16 g
1½ cups bottled zesty Italian salad dressing	360 ml
2 tablespoons extra-virgin olive oil	30 ml

- In small bowl, combine dry dressing mix, bottled dressing and olive oil and mix well.

- Pour over vegetables and toss to coat. Refrigerate several hours before serving or make 1 day in advance.

Ham Salad 1

3 cups cooked, chopped ham	710 ml
1 bunch fresh green onions with tops, chopped	
½ cup slivered almonds, toasted	120 ml
½ cup sunflower seeds	120 ml
2 cups chopped fresh broccoli florets	480 ml
¾ cup mayonnaise	180 ml

- Combine chopped ham, green onions, almonds, sunflower seeds and broccoli florets, toss with mayonnaise and chill. Serve on lettuce leaf.

Ham Salad 2

3 cups cooked, chopped ham	710 ml
¾ cup chopped celery	180 ml
1 cup small-curd cottage cheese, drained	240 ml
1 cup chopped cauliflower florets	240 ml
1 cup chopped broccoli florets	240 ml
Prepared honey-mustard salad dressing	

- Combine ham, celery, cottage cheese, cauliflower and broccoli, toss with salad dressing and chill. Serve on lettuce leaves.

*Vegetable Ham Chowder

A great recipe for leftover ham

1 medium potato	1
1 cup diced ham	1
2 (10 ounce) cans cream of celery soup	2 (280 g)
1 (14 ounce) can chicken broth	1 (396 g)
3 cups finely diced ham	710 ml
1 (15 ounce) can whole kernel corn	1 (425 g)
2 carrots, sliced	2
1 onion, coarsely chopped	1
1 teaspoon dried basil	5 ml
1 (10 ounce) package frozen broccoli florets	1 (280 g)

- Cut potato into 1-inch (2.5 cm) pieces. Combine all ingredients except broccoli florets in large slow cooker.

- Cover and cook on LOW for 5 to 6 hours. Add broccoli and 1 teaspoon (5 ml) each of salt and pepper to cooker and cook for 1 more hour.

Sandwich Souffle

A fun lunch!

Butter, softened
8 slices white bread without crusts
4 slices ham
4 slices American cheese
2 cups milk   480 ml
2 eggs, beaten

- Preheat oven to 350° (176° C). Butter bread on both sides, make 4 sandwiches with ham and cheese. Place sandwiches in buttered 8-inch (20 cm) square baking pan.

- Beat milk, eggs and a little salt and pepper. Pour over sandwiches and soak for 1 to 2 hours.

- Bake for 45-50 minutes.

Sausage Casserole

1 pound pork sausage   .6 kg
2 (15 ounce) cans pork and beans   2 (425 g)
1 (15 ounce) can Mexican-style stewed tomatoes 425 g
1 package corn muffin mix

- Brown sausage and drain fat. Add beans and tomatoes, mix and bring to a boil.

- Pour into 3-quart (3 L) greased casserole. Prepare muffin mix according to package directions. Drop by teaspoonfuls over meat-bean mixture.

- Bake at 400° (204° C) for 30 minutes or until top is brown.

Pork-Stuffed Eggplant

1 large eggplant	
¾ pound ground pork	340 g
½ pound pork sausage	227 g
1 egg	
½ cup dry breadcrumbs	120 ml
½ cup grated romano cheese	120 ml
1 tablespoon dried parsley flakes	15 ml
1 tablespoon dried onion flakes	15 ml
1 teaspoon dried oregano	5 ml
1 (15 ounce) can stewed tomatoes	425 g
1 (8 ounce) can tomato sauce	227 g

- Preheat oven to 350° (176° C). Cut off eggplant stem and cut in half lengthwise. Scoop out and reserve center, leaving a ½-inch (1.2 cm) shell.

- Steam shell halves for about 5 minutes or just until tender. Drain well.

- Cube reserved eggplant and cook in saucepan with boiling salted water for about 6 minutes, drain well and set aside.

- In skillet over medium heat, cook pork and sausage until no longer pink and drain.

- Add eggplant cubes, egg, breadcrumbs, cheese, parsley flakes, onion flakes, oregano, about ½ teaspoon (2 ml) each of salt and pepper and mix well.

- Fill shells and place in greased 7 x 11-inch (18 x 28 cm) baking dish. Pour stewed tomatoes and tomato sauce over eggplant. Cover and bake for 30 minutes.

Loaded Potatoes

6 large baking potatoes, washed
1 (1 pound) bulk pork sausage .5 kg
1 (8 ounce) package cubed processed cheese 227 g
1 (10 ounce) can diced tomatoes and green
   chilies, drained 280 g

- Cook potatoes in microwave until done. Brown sausage in skillet over medium heat and drain fat. Add cheese and diced tomatoes and stir well.

- With knife, cut potatoes down center and fluff insides with fork.

- Spoon generous amounts of sausage-cheese mixture on each potato and reheat in microwave 2 to 3 minutes if necessary.

Italian Sausage and Ravioli

1 pound sweet Italian pork sausage .5 kg
1 (1 pound 10 ounce) jar extra chunky
   mushroom and green pepper spaghetti sauce 737 g
1 (24 ounce) package frozen cheese-filled ravioli,
   cooked, drained 680 g
Grated parmesan cheese

- Remove casing from sausage and cook in large skillet over medium until brown and no longer pink. Stir to separate sausage or slice sausage and drain. Stir in spaghetti sauce and heat to boiling.

- Cook ravioli according to package directions and add to spaghetti and sausage. Sprinkle with parmesan cheese and pour into serving dish.

Zesty Ziti

1 pound Italian sausage links	.5 kg
1 onion, cut into long strips	
1 green bell pepper, julienne	
1 tablespoon oil	15 ml
1 (15 ounce) can diced tomatoes	425 g
1 (15 ounce) can Italian stewed tomatoes	425 g
2 tablespoons ketchup	30 ml
1 (16 ounce) package ziti pasta	.5 kg
1 cup shredded mozzarella cheese	240 ml

- Preheat oven to 350° (176° C).

- Slice sausage into ½-inch (1.2 cm) pieces. Cook sausage, onion and bell pepper in oil over medium heat in large skillet and drain.

- Add diced tomatoes, stewed tomatoes and ketchup and mix well.

- Cook ziti according to package directions and drain.

- In large bowl, combine sausage-onion mixture and tomato mixture and toss with pasta and cheese.

- Spoon into greased 3-quart (3 L) baking dish. Cover and bake from 20 minutes.

*Sausage and Beans

1 (1 pound) fully cooked smoked, link sausage	1 (.5 g)
2 (15 ounce) cans baked beans	2 (425 g)
1 (15 ounce) can great northern beans, drained	425 g
1 (15 ounce) can pinto beans, drained	425 g
½ cup chili sauce	120 ml
⅔ cup packed brown sugar	160 ml
1 tablespoon Worcestershire sauce	15 ml

- Cut link sausage into 1-inch slices. Layer sausage and beans in slow cooker.

- Combine chili sauce, brown sugar, a little black pepper and Worcestershire sauce and pour over beans and sausage.

- Cover and cook in slow cooker on LOW for 4 hours. Stir before serving.

*Indicates slow cooker recipes.

Pizza Pies

½ pound bulk turkey sausage	227 g
⅔ cup prepared pizza sauce	160 ml
1 (10 ounce) package refrigerated pizza dough	280 g
½ cup shredded mozzarella cheese	120 ml

- Preheat oven to 400° (204° C). Brown sausage in skillet and stir to break up pieces of meat.

- Drain fat, add pizza sauce and heat until bubbly.

- Unroll pizza dough, place on flat surface and pat into an 8 x 12-inch (20 x 32 cm) rectangle. Cut into 6 squares.

- Divide sausage mixture evenly among squares and sprinkle with cheese.

- Lift one corner of each square and fold over filling to make triangle.

- Press edges together with tines of fork to seal. Bake about 12 minutes or until light golden brown. Serve immediately.

TIP: Use this short-cut version of pizza or put your favorite ingredients inside - I like "double cheese" on mine, but check your refrigerator for extras. (Additional ingredients may need to be cooked before adding.)

As-Easy-As-Falling-Off-A-Log
Baked Ham

*Yes, it really is that easy! The best part is that people
will rave about it and want to know your recipe.*

**1 (4-5 pound) shank or butt-portion ham   1.8-2.2 kg
Foil**

- Preheat oven to 350° (176° C).

- Unwrap plastic around ham and place in large roasting
  pan. Wrap foil over top and seal edges around pan
  opening.

- Bake for 3 to 3 hours 30 minutes. Remove foil, place
  ham on large platter and slice.

*TIP: This isn't the prettiest cut of pork in the grocery store, but it sure
is tasty. And, when you have sliced the meat off the bone, you have
great seasoning with the bone and meat scraps.*

Easy Baked Chops

**4 (½-1 inch) pork chops   4 (1.2-2.5 cm)
1-2 tablespoons onion soup mix   15-30 ml
2 tablespoons French salad dressing   30 ml**

- Preheat oven to 350° (176° C). Brown pork chops on
  both sides in large skillet with a little oil. Sprinkle soup
  mix over top.

- Pour in salad dressing and ¼ cup (60 ml) cup water.
  Cover and bake for about 1 hour.

Easy Seaworthy Seafood

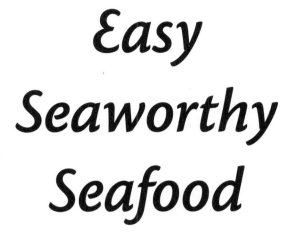

No-Noodle Tuna

1 (8 ounce) tube refrigerated crescent rolls	227 g
1 cup shredded white cheddar cheese	240 ml
1 (10 ounce) box frozen chopped broccoli, thawed	280 g
4 eggs, beaten	
1 (2 ounce) box cream of broccoli soup mix	57 g
1 (8 ounce) carton sour cream	227 g
1 cup milk	240 ml
½ cup mayonnaise	120 ml
2 tablespoons dried onion flakes	30 ml
½ teaspoon dill weed	2 ml
2 (6 ounce) cans white meat tuna, drained, flaked	2 (168 g)
1 (2 ounce) jar diced pimentos	57 g

- Preheat oven to 350° (176° C).

- Unroll crescent roll dough into one long rectangle and place in ungreased 9 x 13-inch (23 x 33 cm) baking dish.

- Seal seams and press on bottom and ½-inch (1.2 cm) up sides. Sprinkle with cheese and chopped broccoli.

- In bowl, combine eggs, broccoli soup mix, sour cream, milk, mayonnaise, onion flakes and dill weed and mix well.

- Stir in tuna and pimentos. Pour over broccoli-cheese in baking dish.

- Bake covered for 40 minutes or until knife inserted near center comes out clean. Cut in squares to serve.

Ever-Ready Tuna Casserole

1 (7 ounce) package elbow macaroni	198 g
1 (8 ounce) package shredded processed cheese	227 g
2 (6 ounce) cans tuna, drained	2 (168 g)
1 (10 ounce) can cream of celery soup	280 g
1 cup milk	240 ml

- Preheat oven to 350° (176° C).

- Cook macaroni according to package directions. Drain well, add cheese and stir until cheese melts.

- Add tuna, celery soup and milk and continue stirring.

- Spoon into greased 7 x 11-inch (18 x 28 cm) baking dish. Cover and bake 35 minutes or until bubbly.

Tuna-Stuffed Tomatoes

4 large tomatoes	
2 (6 ounce) cans white meat tuna, drained	2 (168 g)
2 cups chopped celery	480 ml
½ cup chopped cashews	120 ml
1 small zucchini with peel, finely chopped	
½ cup mayonnaise	120 ml

- Cut thin slice off top of each tomato, scoop out pulp and discard. Turn tomatoes, top down, on paper towels to drain.

- Combine tuna, celery, cashews, zucchini, mayonnaise and a little salt and pepper to taste and mix well. Spoon mixture into hollowed-out tomatoes. Refrigerate.

Skillet Shrimp Scampi

2 teaspoons olive oil	10 ml
2 pounds uncooked shrimp, peeled, veined	1 kg
⅔ cup herb-garlic marinade with lemon juice	160 ml
¼ cup finely chopped green onion with tops	60 ml
Rice or pasta	

- Heat oil in large non-stick skillet. Add shrimp and marinade and cook, stirring often, until shrimp turn pink.

- Stir in green onions. Serve over hot, cooked rice or your favorite pasta.

Ever-Ready Sauce
For Tuna Pasta

Sauce:

1 tablespoon olive oil	15 ml
2 teaspoons minced garlic	10 ml
2 teaspoons sugar	10 ml
¼ teaspoon cayenne pepper	1 ml
2 teaspoons dried basil	10 ml
1 (18 ounce) can stewed tomatoes	510 g

Tuna:

1 (12 ounce) can water-packed tuna, drained	340 g
¾ cup pitted, green olives, sliced	180 ml
¼ cup drained capers	60 ml
1 cup favorite pasta, cooked	240 ml

- Heat olive oil in saucepan and add garlic, sugar, pepper and basil. Cook on low heat for 2 minutes.

- Add stewed tomatoes, bring to boil, reduce heat and simmer 20 minutes.

- In serving bowl, combine tuna, olives, capers and pasta, stir in sauce and toss.

Tuna-Asparagus Pot Pie

1 (8 ounce) package crescent rolls, divided	227 g
1 (6 ounce) can solid white tuna in water, drained	168 g
1 (15 ounce) can cut asparagus, drained	425 ml
1 cup shredded cheddar cheese	240 ml

- Form 7-inch (18 cm) square using 4 crescent rolls.

- Pinch edges together to seal and place in 8 x 8-inch (20 x 20 cm) square sprayed baking pan.

- Spread dough with tuna, then asparagus and shredded cheese.

- Form remaining 4 crescent rolls into 1 square and place on top of cheese.

- Bake at 375° (190° C) for 20 minutes or until top browns and cheese bubbles.

Tuna-In-the-Straw

1 (8 ounce) package egg noodles	227 g
2 (10 ounce) cans cream of chicken soup	2 (280 g)
1 (8 ounce) carton sour cream	227 g
1 teaspoon Creole seasoning	5 ml
½ cup milk	120 ml
2 (6 ounce) cans white meat tuna, drained, flaked	2 (168 g)
1 cup shredded processed cheese	240 ml
1 (10 ounce) box green peas, thawed	280 g
1 (2 ounce) jar diced pimento	57 g
1 (1.5 ounce) can shoestring potatoes	45 g

- Cook noodles according to package directions and drain.

- Combine soup, sour cream, Creole seasoning and milk in large saucepan and mix well.

- Add noodles, tuna, cheese, peas and pimento to saucepan.

- Pour into greased 9 x 13-inch (23 x 33 cm) baking dish.

- Bake uncovered at 350° (176° C) for about 35 minutes or until shoestring potatoes are light brown.

Alfredo Salmon and Noodles

3 cups uncooked medium egg noodles	710 ml
1 (16 ounce) package frozen broccoli florets, thawed	.5 kg
1 cup prepared alfredo sauce	240 ml
1 (15 ounce) can salmon, drained, boned	425 g

• Cook noodles in large saucepan according to package directions. Add broccoli last 5 minutes of cooking time and drain. (Discard broccoli stems.)

• Stir in alfredo sauce and salmon and cook on low heat, stirring occasionally, until mixture heats through. Pour into serving bowl.

TIP: *You can make the alfredo sauce yourself, buy it fresh in the refrigerated section of the grocery store or buy it in a jar. The time is up to you.*

Two ounces dry pasta will make about 1 cup cooked pasta. Spaghetti and macaroni products usually double in volume when cooked. Egg noodles don't expand quite as much.

Pan-Fried Flounder

1 tablespoon and 1 teaspoon seafood seasoning	15 ml; 5 ml
¼ teaspoon cayenne pepper	1 ml
⅔ cup flour	160 ml
¼ cup olive oil	60 ml
6-8 small flounder fillets	
¾ cup prepared tartar sauce	180 ml
⅓ cup ketchup	80 ml

- Combine 1 tablespoon (15 ml) seafood seasoning, cayenne pepper, about ¼ teaspoon (1 ml) pepper, flour and ½ teaspoon (2 ml) salt.

- Heat oil over high heat in large skillet. Dredge each fillet in flour-seasoning mixture and place in skillet (in batches). Fry about 3 minutes on each side, depending on thickness of fillets. Drain on paper towels.

- Combine tartar sauce, ketchup and 1 teaspoon (5 ml) seafood seasoning and serve with fried flounder.

Sunday Best Fried Fish

1 (16 ounce) package frozen, cooked, batter-dipped fried fish	.5 kg
1 cup prepared spaghetti sauce	240 ml
2 teaspoons Italian seasoning	10 ml
1 cup shredded mozzarella cheese	240 ml

- Heat fish according to package directions. While fish is heating, combine spaghetti sauce and Italian seasoning.

- When fish heats thoroughly, place each piece on serving plate and spoon spaghetti mixture over fish. Sprinkle cheese on top and serve.

Broiled Red Snapper

2 tablespoons dijon-style mustard	30 ml
¼ cup Italian salad dressing	60 ml
4 (6 ounce) red snapper fillets	4 (168 g)

- Preheat broiler. Combine mustard and Italian dressing in small bowl. Place snapper, skin side down, on foil-lined baking pan sprayed with cooking oil.

- Brush mustard-dressing mixture over fillets and broil about 8 minutes or until snapper flakes easily when tested with fork.

Grilled Swordfish With Pepper Sauce

4 (1-inch) swordfish steaks	4 (2.5 cm)
3 tablespoons olive oil	45 ml
½ teaspoon lemon pepper	2 ml

Sauce:
⅓ cup roasted red pepper	80 ml
1 tablespoon dijon-style mustard	15 ml
3 tablespoons mayonnaise	45 ml

- Rub swordfish with olive oil and sprinkle with ¾ teaspoon (4 ml) salt and lemon pepper.

- Grill over medium to high heat for about 10 minutes turn once or until it cooks thoroughly. (Do not overcook. It will dry fish out.)

- Place all sauce ingredients plus ½ teaspoon (2 ml) pepper in blender and process until they blend well. Serve over grilled swordfish.

Extra-Special Fried Fish

1 (16 ounce) package frozen, cooked batter-dipped fried fish	.5 kg
¾ cup chili sauce	180 ml
1 bunch fresh green onions, chopped	
1 cup shredded cheddar cheese	240 ml

- Preheat oven to 325° (162° C). Arrange fish in greased
  9 x 13-inch (23 x 33 cm) glass baking dish and heat
  about 20 minutes or just until fish heats thoroughly.

- Heat chili sauce in saucepan and spoon over each piece
  of fish. Top with chopped green onions and cheddar
  cheese. Serve right from baking dish.

Red Snapper with Fresh Salsa

6 (6 ounce) red snapper fillets	6 (168 g)
1 teaspoon ground cumin	5 ml
½ teaspoon cayenne pepper	2 ml

Salsa:

½ cup chopped fresh cilantro	120 ml
1 (15 ounce) can great northern beans, drained	425 g
1 (15 ounce) can Italian stewed tomatoes, drained	425 g
⅓ cup chopped green olives	80 ml
1 teaspoon minced garlic	5 ml

- Dry snapper with paper towels and rub a little oil on
  both sides of snapper. Sprinkle with cumin, cayenne
  pepper and ½ teaspoon (2 ml) salt.

- Grill snapper about 5 minutes on each side or until
  fish flakes easily when tested with fork. Combine fresh
  cilantro, beans, tomatoes, olives and minced garlic and
  mix well. Serve with each red snapper and garnish with
  slice of fresh lime, if you like.

Salmon and Green Beans

4 (6 ounce) salmon steaks	4 (168 g)
¼ cup lite soy sauce	60 ml
2 tablespoons lemon juice	15 ml
1 (10 ounce) package frozen whole green beans	280 g

- Place a little oil in skillet over medium to high heat and add salmon steaks. Combine soy sauce and lemon juice and pour over steaks.

- Cover and cook about 5 minutes. Turn salmon and place green beans over salmon with 2 tablespoons (30 ml) water.

- Cover and steam 5 minutes or until beans are tender-crisp. Season green beans with a little salt and pepper and serve over hot buttered rice.

Shrimp Newburg

1 (10 ounce) can cream of shrimp soup	280 g
1 teaspoon seafood seasoning	5 ml
1 (1 pound) package frozen cooked salad shrimp, thawed	.5 kg

- Combine soup, ¼ cup (60 ml) water and seafood seasoning in saucepan. Bring to boil, reduce heat and stir in shrimp.

- Heat thoroughly and serve over hot white rice.

Salmon Casserole

1 (6 ounce) package dried egg noodles	168 g
1 (10 ounce) can cream of celery soup	280 g
1 (5 ounce) can evaporated milk	143 g
1 tablespoon lemon juice	15 ml
½ onion, chopped	
1 (15 ounce) can salmon, skinned, boned	425 g
1 cup shredded cheddar cheese	240 ml
1 (8 ounce) can small green peas, drained	227 g
½ teaspoon Creole seasoning	2 ml
1 cup crushed cheese crackers	240 ml
2 tablespoons butter, melted	30 ml

- Cook noodles according to package directions and drain. Preheat oven to 350° (176° C).

- Stir in soup, milk, lemon juice, onion, salmon, cheese, Creole seasoning, peas, ¼ teaspoon (1 ml) each of salt and pepper.

- Spoon into greased 7 x 11-inch (18 x 28 cm) baking dish. Bake covered for 25 minutes.

- Combine cheese crackers and melted butter and sprinkle over casserole.

- Return to oven for 10 minutes or until crumbs are light brown.

Thai Peanut Noodles

1 (5.5 ounce) box Thai stir-fry rice noodles with seasoning packet	155 g
1 pound peeled, veined shrimp	.5 kg
1 (10 ounce) package frozen broccoli florets, thawed	280 g
½ cup peanuts	120 ml

- Boil 3 cups (710 ml) water in saucepan and stir in noodles.

- Turn heat off and soak noodles about 5 minutes. Drain and rinse in cold water.

- Saute shrimp and broccoli in skillet with a little oil for about 8 minutes or just until shrimp turns pink.

- Add softened noodles, seasoning packet and peanuts. (There are chopped peanuts in seasoning, but this dish is better, if you add more peanuts.)

TIP: If noodles are still too firm after they soak, add 1 tablespoon (15 ml) water and stir-fry until noodles are tender.

Savory Shrimp Fetuccine

2 tablespoons butter	30 ml
⅓ cup chopped onion	80 ml
1 teaspoon seafood seasoning	5 ml
½ pound small shrimp, peeled, veined	227 g
1 (10 ounce) can cream of shrimp soup	280 g
½ cup half-and-half cream	120 ml
½ cup mayonnaise	120 ml
2 teaspoons white wine Worcestershire sauce	10 ml
½ teaspoon prepared horseradish	2 ml
1 cup grated white cheddar cheese, divided	240 ml
2 cups cooked fettuccine	480 ml
1 (16 ounce) package frozen broccoli florets, cooked	.5 kg

- In large saucepan, melt butter and saute onion. Add seasoning and shrimp and cook, while stirring, until shrimp turn pink, about 2 minutes.

- Add shrimp soup, cream, mayonnaise, Worcestershire, horseradish and half the cheese. Heat just until cheese melts. Fold in fettuccine.

- When broccoli cools from cooking, cut some stems away and discard. Fold broccoli into sauce. Preheat oven to 350° (176° C).

- Spoon into buttered 3-quart (3 L) baking dish. Cover and bake for 30 minutes.

- Remove from oven and sprinkle remaining cheese on top. Bake 5 minutes longer.

Fettuccine of the Sea

¼ cup (½ stick) butter	60 ml
¼ cup flour	60 ml
1 teaspoon Creole seasoning	5 ml
1 tablespoon minced garlic	15 ml
1 (16 ounce) carton half-and-half cream	.5 kg
½ cup milk	120 ml
½ cup finely chopped red bell pepper	120 ml
2 (6 ounce) cans tiny shrimp, picked, veined	2 (168 g)
2 (6 ounce) cans crabmeat, picked, drained	2 (168 g)
1 (6 ounce) can chopped clams, drained	168 g
½ cup grated parmesan cheese	120 ml
1 (12 ounce) package fettuccine, cooked al dente	340 g

- Preheat oven to 325° (162° C).

- In saucepan, melt butter and add flour, Creole seasoning, garlic, ¾ teaspoon (4 ml) pepper and mix well.

- On medium heat, gradually add cream and milk and mix well. Cook, stirring constantly, until it thickens.

- Add bell pepper, shrimp, crabmeat, clams and parmesan cheese and heat thoroughly.

- In buttered 9 x 13-inch (23 x 33 cm) baking dish, spoon half fettuccine in bottom of dish and half seafood sauce. Repeat layers.

- Cover and bake for 25 minutes or just until casserole is bubbly. To serve, sprinkle parsley over top of casserole.

Crab-Stuffed Baked Potatoes

This potato is truly a meal in itself!

4 large baking potatoes	
½ cup (1 stick) butter	120 ml
½ cup whipping cream	120 ml
1 bunch fresh green onions, chopped	
2 (6 ounce) cans crabmeat, drained, flaked	2 (168 g)
¾ cup shredded cheddar cheese	180 ml
2 tablespoons fresh minced parsley	30 ml

- Bake potatoes at 375° (190° C) for 1 hour or until well done.

- Halve each potato lengthwise and scoop out pulp, but leave skins intact.

- In large bowl, mash potatoes with butter.

- Add whipping cream, ¾ teaspoon (4 ml) salt, ½ teaspoon (2 ml) pepper and green onions. Stir in crabmeat.

- Fill reserved potato skins with potato mixture. Sprinkle with cheese.

- Bake 350° (176° C) for about 15 minutes. To serve, sprinkle fresh parsley over cheese.

Creamed Shrimp-Over-Rice

3 (10 ounce) cans frozen cream of shrimp soup   3 (280 g)
1 pint sour cream   .5 kg
1½ teaspoons curry powder   7 ml
2 (5 ounce) cans veined shrimp   2 (143 g)
Rice, cooked

- Combine all ingredients in double boiler. Heat and stir constantly but do not boil.

- Serve over hot cooked rice.

Shrimp in Sour Cream

2 green onions, chopped
8 ounces fresh mushrooms, washed, drained,
   sliced   227 g
2 tablespoons butter   10ml
1 pound (18 to 22 count) shrimp, cooked,
   peeled, cleaned   .5 kg
1 tablespoon flour   15 ml
1 teaspoon Worcestershire suce   5 ml
2 tablespoons dry sherry   30 ml
1 (8 ounce) carton sour cream   227 g
Cooked rice

- In skillet, saute green onions and mushrooms in butter for 5 minutes.

- Add shrimp and heat. Sprinkle mixture with flour, Worcestershire, ½ teaspoon (2 ml) each of salt and pepper. Add sherry and sour cream, mix well.

- Cook over low heat until hot, but do not let boil. Serve over cooked rice.

Easy
Desserts

Sweet Angel Cake

This gets rave reviews whenever I serve it. It's one of my favorites.

1½ cups powdered sugar	360 ml
⅓ cup milk	80 ml
1 (8 ounce) package cream cheese, softened	227 g
1 (3½ ounce) can flaked coconut	100 g
1 cup chopped pecans	240 ml
1 (12 ounce) carton whipped topping	340 g
1 large angel food cake, torn into bite-size pieces	
1 (16 ounce) can cherry pie filling	.5 kg

- Add sugar and milk to cream cheese and beat in mixer. Fold in coconut and pecans, stir in whipped topping and cake pieces.

- Spread in large 9 x 13-inch (23 x 33 cm) glass dish and chill for several hours.

- Add pie filling by tablespoon on top of cake mixture. (It will not cover cake mixture, but it will just be in clumps, making a pretty red and white dessert.) Chill. Serves 15 to 16.

Chocolate Hurricane Cake

This is easy and very, very yummy.

1 cup chopped pecans	240 ml
1 (3 ounce) can sweetened flaked coconut	84 g
1 (18 ounce) box German chocolate cake mix	510 g
⅓ cup oil	80 ml
3 eggs	
½ cup (1 stick) butter, melted	120 ml
1 (8 ounce) package cream cheese, softened	227 g
1 (16 ounce) box powdered sugar	.5 kg

- Preheat oven to 350° (176° C).

- Spray 9 x 13-inch (23 x 33 cm) baking pan. Cover bottom of pan with pecans and coconut.

- In mixing bowl, combine cake mix, 1¼ cups (300 ml) water, oil and eggs and beat well.

- Carefully pour batter over pecans and coconut.

- Combine butter, cream cheese and powdered sugar in mixing bowl and whip to blend.

- Spoon mixture over unbaked batter and bake for 40 to 42 minutes.

TIP: You cannot test for doneness with cake tester or toothpick because cake will appear sticky even when it is done. The icing sinks into bottom as it bakes and forms white ribbon inside.

Turtle Cake Wow!

1 (18 ounce) box German chocolate cake mix	510 g
½ cup (1 stick) butter, softened	120 ml
½ cup oil	120 ml
1 (14 ounce) can sweetened, condensed milk, divided	396 g
1 (1 pound) bag caramels	.5 kg
1 cup chopped pecans	240 ml

- Preheat oven to 350° (176° C).

- Combine cake mix, butter, 1½ cups (360 ml) water, oil and half condensed milk.

- Pour half batter into sprayed 9 x 13-inch (23 x 33 cm) pan and bake for 20 minutes.

- Melt caramels and blend with remaining condensed milk. Spread evenly over baked cake layer and sprinkle with pecans. Cover with remaining batter and bake an additional 20 to 25 minutes.

Icing:

½ cup (1 stick) butter	120 ml
3 tablespoons cocoa	45 ml
6 tablespoons evaporated milk	90 ml
1 (16 ounce) box powdered sugar	.5 kg
1 teaspoon vanilla	5 ml

- Melt butter in saucepan and mix in cocoa and milk.

- Add powdered sugar and vanilla to mixture and blend well. Spread over cake. Serves 24.

Coconut-Cake Deluxe

*This cake is really moist and delicious and
can be frozen if you need to make it in advance.*

1 (18 ounce) box yellow cake mix	510 g
1 (14 ounce) can sweetened, condensed milk	396 g
1 (15 ounce) can coconut cream	425 g
1 (3 ounce) can flaked coconut	84 g
1 (8 ounce) carton whipped topping	227 g

- Preheat oven to 350° (176° C).

- Prepare cake mix according to package directions and pour into sprayed 9 x 13-inch (23 x 33 cm) baking pan.

- Bake for 30 to 35 minutes or until toothpick inserted in center comes out clean.

- While cake is warm, punch holes in cake about 2 inches apart.

- Pour condensed milk over cake and spread around until all milk soaks into cake.

- Pour coconut cream over cake and sprinkle coconut on top.

- Cool and frost with whipped topping. Serves 12 to 15.

Easy Breezy Pineapple Cake

2 cups sugar	480 ml
2 cups flour	480 ml
1 (20 ounce) can crushed pineapple with juice	567 g
1 teaspoon baking soda	5 ml
1 teaspoon vanilla	5 ml

- Preheat oven to 350° (176° C).

- Combine all cake ingredients and ½ teaspoon (2 ml) salt and mix well by hand.

- Pour into sprayed 9 x 13-inch (23 x 33 cm) baking pan and bake for 30 to 35 minutes.

Icing:

1 (8 ounce) package cream cheese, softened	227 g
½ cup (1 stick) butter, melted	120 ml
1 cup powdered sugar	240 ml
1 cup chopped pecans	240 ml

- To prepare icing, beat all ingredients except pecans with mixer.

- Add pecans, stir to mix well and spread icing over hot cake.

Oreo Cake

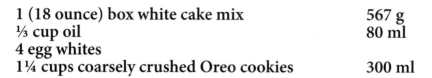

1 (18 ounce) box white cake mix	567 g
⅓ cup oil	80 ml
4 egg whites	
1¼ cups coarsely crushed Oreo cookies	300 ml

- Preheat oven to 350° (176° C). Spray 2 (8 or 9-inch/ 23 cm) round cake pans.

- Combine cake mix, 1¼ cups (300 ml) water, oil and egg whites in large mixing bowl. Blend on low speed until moist.

- Beat for 2 minutes at high speed and gently fold in coarsely crushed cookies.

- Pour batter into prepared pans and bake for 25 to 30 minutes or until toothpick inserted in center comes out clean. Cool for 10 minutes, remove from pan and cool.

Icing:

4¼ cups powdered sugar	1.1 L
1 cup (2 sticks) butter, softened	240 ml
1 cup shortening*	240 ml
1 teaspoon almond flavoring	5 ml
¼ cup crushed Oreo cookies	60 ml
¼ cup chopped pecans	60 ml

- Beat all ingredients except crushed cookie pieces and pecans. Frost first layer, place second layer on top and frost top and sides. Sprinkle crushed Oreo cookies and pecans on top.

*TIP: The butter-flavored shortening is not the best for this recipe, so stick to the regular unflavored shortening.

Piña Colada Cake

1 (18 ounce) box orange cake mix	510 g
3 eggs	
⅓ cup oil	80 ml
1 (14 ounce) can sweetened, condensed milk	396 g
1 (15 ounce) can coconut cream	425 g
1 cup flaked coconut	240 ml
1 (8 ounce) can crushed pineapple, drained	227 g
1 (8 ounce) carton whipped topping	227 g

- Preheat oven to 350° (176° C). Combine cake mix, eggs, 1¼ cups (300 ml) water and oil in mixing bowl. Beat for 3 or 4 minutes and pour into deep, greased, floured 10 x 14-inch (25 x 36 cm) baking pan.

- Bake for 35 minutes. When cake is done, punch holes in cake with fork so frosting will soak into cake.

- Mix condensed milk, coconut cream, coconut and pineapple. While cake is warm, pour mixture over cake. Chill until cake is cold, spread layer of whipped topping over cake and return to refrigerator.

Pecan Pie

2 tablespoons flour	30 ml
3 tablespoons butter, melted	45 ml
3 eggs, beaten	
⅔ cup sugar	160 ml
1 cup corn syrup	240 ml
1 teaspoon vanilla	5 ml
1 cup chopped pecans	240 ml
1 (9-inch) unbaked piecrust	23 cm

- Preheat oven to 350° (176° C). Combine flour, butter, eggs, sugar, corn syrup and vanilla in mixing bowl and mix well.

- Place pecans in piecrust and pour egg mixture over pecans.

- Bake for 10 minutes, reduce heat to 275° (135° C) and bake for 50 to 55 minutes or until center of pie is fairly firm.

TIP: Recipe ingredient variations include using 2 tablespoons (30 ml) amaretto instead of vanilla. Also you could add 1 teaspoon (5 ml) cinnamon and ½ teaspoon (2 ml) nutmeg to recipe.

Creamy Lemon Pie

1 (8 ounce) package cream cheese, softened	227 g
1 (14 ounce) can sweetened, condensed milk	396 g
1/4 cup lemon juice	60 ml
1 (20 ounce) can lemon pie filling	567 g
1 (9-inch) graham cracker piecrust	23 cm

- Beat cream cheese in mixing bowl until smooth and creamy. Add condensed milk and lemon juice and beat until mixture is creamy.

- Fold in lemon pie filling and stir well. Pour into piecrust and chill several hours before slicing and serving.

Kahula Pie

26 marshmallows	
1 (13 ounce) can evaporated milk	369 g
1 (1 ounce) package unflavored gelatin	28 g
1 (8 ounce) carton whipping cream	227 g
½ cup kahula	120 ml
1 (9-inch) chocolate cookie piecrust	23 cm
Chocolate curls	

- Melt marshmallows with evaporated milk in saucepan over low to medium heat. Stir constantly and do not let milk boil.

- Dissolve gelatin in ¼ cup (60 ml) cold water. Remove marshmallows mixture from heat and add dissolved gelatin. Chill until mixture thickens slightly.

- Whip cream and fold into marshmallow mixture. Mix in kahula and pour into piecrust. Garnish with chocolate and curls and chill overnight.

Dream Pie

1 (8 ounce) package cream cheese, softened	227 g
1 (14 ounce) can sweetened, condensed milk	396 g
1 (5.1 ounce) package vanilla	
instant pudding mix	145 g
1 (8 ounce) carton whipped topping	227 g
2 (9-inch) graham cracker ready piecrusts	2 (23 cm)
1 (20 ounce) can strawberry pie filling	567 g

- Beat cream cheese and condensed milk in mixing bowl until smooth. Add pudding mix and ½ cup (120 ml) water, mix and chill for 15 minutes.

- Fold in whipped topping, pour into 2 piecrusts and freeze.

- When ready to serve, remove from freezer and place in refrigerator for 45 minutes before slicing and serving. Spoon about ¼ cup (60 ml) pie filling on each slice of pie. (You could use other pie filling flavors if you like.)

TIP: Here's another version of the same cake.
Use 2 chocolate ready-piecrusts.
Pour 2 or 3 tablespoons (30 ml) chocolate ice cream
topping over pie and top with chocolate shavings.

Outa-Sight Pie

1 (14 ounce) can sweetened, condensed milk	396 g
1 (20 ounce) can lemon pie filling	567 g
1 (20 ounce) can crushed pineapple, drained	567 g
1 (8 ounce) carton whipped topping	227 g
2 (9-inch) cookie-flavored ready piecrusts	2 (23 cm)

- Combine condensed milk, lemon pie filling and pineapple in saucepan over low to medium heat and mix well.

- Fold in whipped topping and pour mixture into 2 piecrusts. Chill several hours before serving.

Peach-Mousse Pie

1 (9-inch) graham cracker piecrust	23 cm
1 (16 ounce) package frozen peach slices, thawed	.5 kg
1 cup sugar	240 ml
1 (1 ounce) package unflavored gelatin	28 ml
⅛ teaspoon ground nutmeg	.5 ml
Yellow and red food coloring	
1 (12 ounce) carton whipped topping	340 g
Nectarine slices for garnish	

- Place peaches in blender and process until peaches are smooth. Pour into saucepan, bring to boil and stir constantly. Remove from burner.

- Combine sugar, gelatin and nutmeg and stir into hot puree until sugar and gelatin dissolve. Pour gelatin mixture into large bowl and place in freezer for 20 minutes or until mixture mounds. Stir occasionally.

- Use mixer to beat gelatin mixture on HIGH speed for 5 minutes or until light and fluffy. Add a few drops of coloring, fold in whipped topping and pour into piecrust.

Apricot Cobbler

*A bridge partner had this recently and everybody gave
it a blue ribbon. This is another one of those recipes
that is really quick and easy plus really delicious.*

1 (20 ounce) can apricot pie filling	567 g
1 (20 ounce) can crushed pineapple with juice	567 g
1 cup chopped pecans	240 ml
1 (18 ounce) box yellow cake mix	510 g
1 cup (2 sticks) butter, melted	240 ml
Whipped topping	

- Preheat oven to 375° (190° C). Pour apricot pie filling
  into sprayed 9 x 13-inch (23 x 33 cm) baking dish and
  spread evenly.

- Spoon crushed pineapple and juice over pie filling.
  Sprinkle pecans over pineapple, then sprinkle cake mix
  over pecans.

- Pour melted butter over cake mix and bake for
  40 minutes or until light brown and crunchy.
  To serve, top with whipped topping. Serves 10.

Seven-Layer Cookies

½ cup (1 stick) butter	120 ml
1 cup crushed graham crackers	240 ml
1 (6 ounce) package semi-sweet chocolate bits	168 g
1 (6 ounce) package butterscotch bits	168 g
1 (3 ounce) can flaked coconut	84 g
1 (14 ounce) can sweetened, condensed milk	396 g
1 cup chopped pecans	240 ml

- Preheat oven to 350° (176° C). Melt butter in 9 x 13-inch (23 x 33 cm) baking pan. Sprinkle remaining ingredients in order listed.

- Do not stir or mix and bake for 30 minutes. Cool before cutting.

Easy Blonde Brownies

This is another one of those recipes that seems too easy to be a recipe – and you already have everything right in the pantry. These brownies are so good and chewy.

1 (1 pound) box light brown sugar	.5 kg
4 eggs	
2 cups biscuit mix	480 ml
2 cups chopped pecans	480 ml

- Preheat oven to 350° (176° C). Use mixer to beat brown sugar, eggs and biscuit mix. Stir in pecans.

- Pour into greased 9 x 13-inch (23 x 33 cm) baking pan. Bake for 35 minutes. Cool and cut into squares.

Snappy Treats

3 cups quick-rolled oats	710 ml
1 cup chocolate chips	240 ml
½ cup flaked coconut	120 ml
½ cup chopped pecans	120 ml
2 cups sugar	480 ml
¾ cup (1½ sticks) butter	180 ml
½ cup evaporated milk	120 ml

- Combine oats, chocolate chips, coconut and pecans in large bowl. In saucepan, boil sugar, butter and milk for 1 to 2 minutes and stir constantly.

- Pour hot mixture over oat-chocolate mixture in bowl and stir until chocolate chips melt.

- Drop by teaspoonfuls on wax paper. Cool at room temperature and store in covered container.

TIP: Use white chocolate chips and ¾ cup (180 ml) candied, cut-up cherries for a colorful variation.

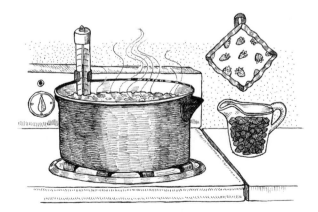

Pecan Squares

2 cups flour	480 ml
½ cup powdered sugar	120 ml
1 cup (2 sticks) butter, cut up	240 ml
1 (14 ounce) can sweetened, condensed milk	396 g
2 eggs	
1 teaspoon vanilla	5 ml
1 (7 ounce) package Bits O'Brickle chips	198 g
1 cup chopped pecans	240 ml

- Preheat oven to 350° (176° C). Combine flour and powdered sugar in medium bowl and mix well. Cut in butter with pastry blender or fork until crumbly.

- Press mixture evenly into sprayed 9 x 13-inch (23 x 33 cm) baking pan and bake for 15 minutes.

- Combine condensed milk, eggs, vanilla, Bits O'Brickle and chopped pecans and pour over prepared crust. Bake for 25 minutes or until golden brown.

- Cool and cut into squares. Makes 4 dozen.

Buttery Walnut Squares

1 cup (2 sticks) butter, softened	240 ml
1¾ cups packed brown sugar	420 ml
1¾ cups flour	420 ml

- Preheat oven to 350° (176° C). Combine butter and sugar and beat until smooth and creamy. Add flour and mix well.

- Pat mixture down evenly in sprayed 9 x 13-inch (23 x 33 cm) glass pan and bake for 15 minutes.

Topping:

1 cup packed brown sugar	120 ml
4 eggs, lightly beaten	
2 tablespoons flour	30 ml
2 cups chopped walnuts	480 ml
1 cup flaked coconut	240 ml

- Combine sugar and eggs in medium bowl. Add flour and mix well.

- Fold in walnuts and coconut and pour over crust. Bake for 20 to 25 minutes or until set in center. Cool in pan and cut into squares.

TIP: Serve these delicious squares with a scoop of ice cream for a great dessert.

Lemon-Angel Bars

1 (1 pound) package 1-step angel food cake mix	.5 kg
1 (20 ounce) can lemon pie filling	567 g
⅓ cup (⅔ stick) butter, softened	80 ml
2 cups powdered sugar	480 ml
2 tablespoons lemon juice	30 ml

- Preheat oven to 350° (176 ° C). Combine cake mix and lemon pie filling in bowl and stir to mix well.

- Pour into sprayed 9 x 13-inch (23 x 33 cm) baking pan and bake for 20 minutes or until done. Remove cake from oven just before cake is done.

- Combine butter, powdered sugar and lemon juice and spread over hot layer. Cake will sink down a little in middle, so make sure icing is on edges of cake as well as in middle.

- When cool, cut into 18 to 24 bars and store in refrigerator. Bars can be served at room temperature or cold.

Fruit Fajitas

1 (20 ounce) can prepared fruit pie filling	567 g
10 small or large flour tortillas	
1½ cups sugar	360 ml
¾ cup (1½ sticks) butter	180 ml
1 teaspoon almond flavoring	5 ml

- Preheat oven to 350° (176° C). Divide fruit equally on tortillas, roll up and place in 9 x 13-inch (23 x 33 cm) baking dish. Combine 2 cups (480 ml) water, sugar and butter in saucepan and bring to a boil.

- Add almond flavoring and pour mixture over flour tortillas. Place in refrigerator and let soak 1 to 24 hours. Bake for 20 to 25 minutes until brown and bubbly.

Oreo Sundae

½ cup (1 stick) butter	120 ml
1 (19 ounce) package Oreo cookies, crushed	538 g
½ gallon vanilla ice cream, softened	1.9 L
2 (12 ounce) jars fudge sauce	2 (340 g)
1 (12 ounce) carton whipped topping	340 g
Maraschino cherries	

- Melt butter in 9 x 13-inch (23 x 33 cm) pan. Mix crushed Oreos (except for ½ cup/120 ml for topping) with butter to form crust. Pour mixture in pan and press down.

- Spread softened ice cream over crust and add layer of fudge sauce. Top with whipped topping and reserved crumbs. Garnish with cherries and freeze until ready to serve. Serves 12.

Lemon Lush

1¼ cups flour	300 ml
⅔ cup (⅓ stick) butter	160 ml
½ cup chopped pecans	120 ml
1 cup powdered sugar	240 ml
1 (8 ounce) package cream cheese, softened	227 g
1 (12 ounce) carton whipped topping, divided	340 g
2 (3.4 ounce) packages instant lemon pudding	2 (100 g)
1 tablespoon lemon juice	15 ml
2¾ cups milk	660 ml

- Preheat oven to 375° (176° C). Combine flour, butter and pecans and pat down into 9 x 13-inch (23 x 33 cm) baking dish. Bake for 15 minutes.

- Beat powdered sugar and cream cheese until fluffy and fold in 2 cups (480 ml) whipped topping. Spread mixture over nut crush.

- Combine pudding, lemon juice and milk and beat. Spread over second layer. Top with remaining whipped topping and chill. To serve, cut into squares.

Index

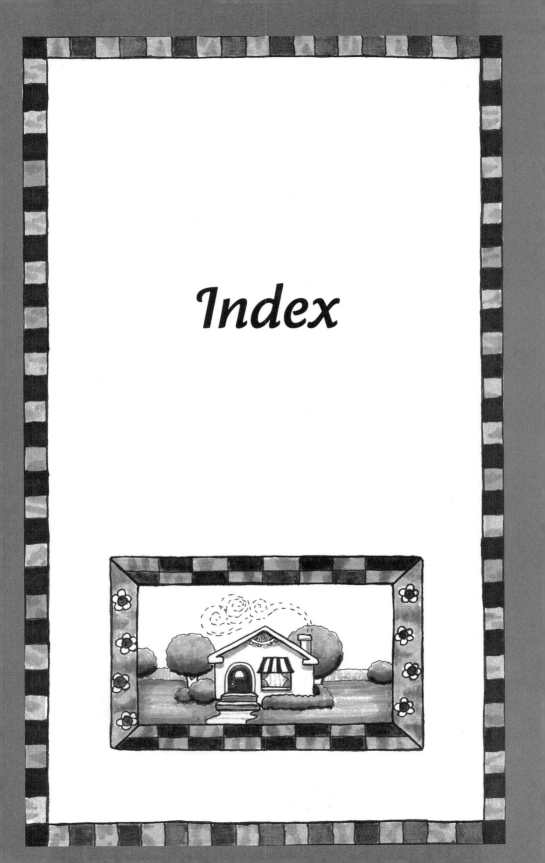

Index

Index

Index

Index

R

S

SALADS

SANDWICHES

SEAFOOD

Index

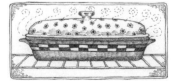